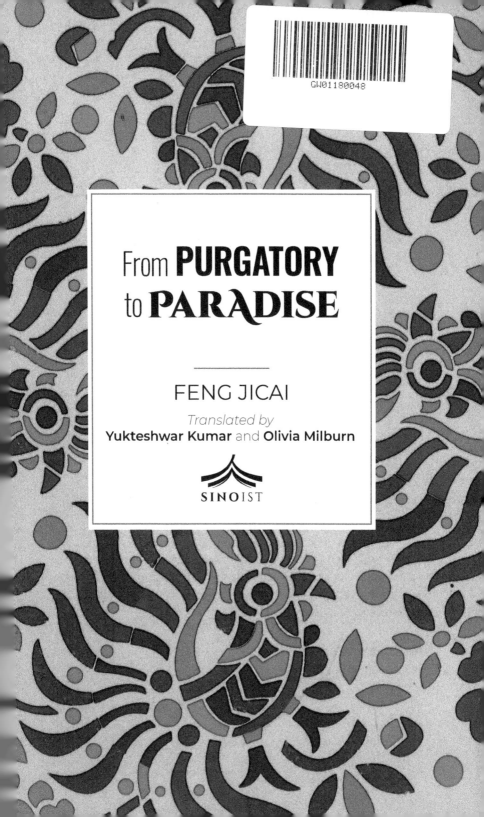

From **PURGATORY** to **PARADISE**

FENG JICAI

Translated by
Yukteshwar Kumar and **Olivia Milburn**

SINOIST

ACA Publishing Ltd
University House
11-13 Lower Grosvenor Place,
London SW1W 0EX, UK
Tel: +44 20 3289 3885
E-mail: info@alaincharlesasia.com
www.alaincharlesasia.com
www.sinoistbooks.com

Beijing Office
Tel: +86(0)10 8472 1250

Author: Feng Jicai
Translators: Yukteshwar Kumar and Olivia Milburn

Published by Sinoist Books (an imprint of ACA Publishing Ltd)

Original Chinese Text © 炼狱·天堂 韩美林口述史 *(Lian Yu Tian Tang Han Mei Lin Kou Shu Shi) 2016,* People's Literature Publishing House, Beijing, China

English Translation text © 2022 ACA Publishing Ltd, London, UK

ALL RIGHTS RESERVED. NO PART OF THIS PUBLICATION MAY BE REPRODUCED IN MATERIAL FORM, BY ANY MEANS, WHETHER GRAPHIC, ELECTRONIC, MECHANICAL OR OTHER, INCLUDING PHOTOCOPYING OR INFORMATION STORAGE, IN WHOLE OR IN PART, AND MAY NOT BE USED TO PREPARE OTHER PUBLICATIONS WITHOUT WRITTEN PERMISSION FROM THE PUBLISHER.

Paperback ISBN: 978-1-83890-538-5
eBook ISBN: 978-1-83890-539-2

A catalogue record for *From Purgatory to Paradise: An Oral History of Artist Han Meilin from the Cultural Revolution to the Present Day* is available from the National Bibliographic Service of the British Library.

FROM PURGATORY TO PARADISE

An Oral History of Artist Han Meilin
from the Cultural Revolution to the Present Day

FENG JICAI

Main text translated by
YUKTESHWAR KUMAR

Appendix translated by
OLIVIA MILBURN

SINOIST BOOKS

CONTENTS

Preface	vii
Foreword	xi

PART ONE
PURGATORY

1. OVERTURE OF SUFFERING	3
1: Misfortune Emanating from the Mouth	3
2: Traitor	12
3: Nine Regions, Eighteen Posts	20
4: 7 April 1967	30
5: Nine Days	41
2. HISTORY OF PURGATORY	49
1: No. 100, Dongshan	49
2: Eighteen Layers of Hell	58
3: Female Prisoners	69
4: Fake Shooting	76
5: The Last Three Sentences	84
3. RETURNING TO THE HUMAN WORLD AGAIN	105
1: The Human World	105
2: Light and Shadow	112

PART TWO
PARADISE

CONVERSATIONS IN THE KINGDOM OF ART	123
1. AN INQUEST INTO THE KINGDOM OF ART	129
2. TRICOLOUR	158
Ancient, Folk and Modern	

3. FOUR BROTHERS   181
Painting, Esoteric Writing, Sculpture and Design

  1: Painting   181
  2: Esoteric Writing   193
  3: Sculpture   200
  4: Design   209

4. ONE MAN'S MOGAO CAVES   214

  Appendix   223
  Endnotes   253
  About Sinoist Books   260
  About the Author   261
  About the Translator   262
  About the Translator   263

PREFACE

LET ME BE VERY HONEST FROM THE OUTSET! Although, I have studied China, Chinese and Chinese culture for more than thirty years, I had not heard of Professor Feng Jicai until 2013. I am deeply ashamed of this. Such a great scholar— I knew nothing about him, but this is a fact.

Twenty years ago, while researching as a Nehru fellow at Peking University, I used to meet Professor Ji Xianlin regularly. He gave me his book *Memories from the Cowshed*. I was particularly moved and shocked by his narratives of the Cultural Revolution in that book. However, that shock was nothing compared to what I came across later in the books authored by Professor Feng Jicai.

I learnt about Professor Feng Jicai through a famous Chinese writer, Xue Xinran. She asked me to organise a lecture by Professor Feng at the University of Bath in 2013, and I readily agreed. On 18 April 2013, in my opening speech while welcoming Professor Feng at the University of Bath, I said: "When Tagore visited China in 1924, Mr Ji Xianlin went

PREFACE

to Jinan to listen to his speech when he was only 13 years old. Now you have come to the UK to speak. I have brought my eight-year-old son to listen to your speech and let him learn from you." At that time, hundreds of students attended his lecture.

In October 2013, Professor Feng invited me to participate in an international conference at his institute in Tianjin. During the meeting, I met Master Han Meilin for the first time. I had heard the name of master artist Han Meilin and knew about his monumental works, but this was the first time I had met him. At that time, I had not realised that one day I would be lucky enough to translate and publish Professor Feng Jicai's book on Han Meilin.

I also know that Professor Feng Jicai's works have been translated into many languages but, in fact, in the West or other English-speaking countries, such as India or Australia, very few people have a deep understanding of Feng Jicai's works.

In March 2018, I visited Beijing again in relation with academic works and sent a letter to Master Han Meilin's secretary, requesting if I could visit his museum. Master Han readily agreed. I went to visit him with Mr Huang Qiang, who is like my brother in China. This great artist personally took me to visit his colossal museum and explained many things related to his art gallery.

In our conversation, we discussed his exhibitions in many countries and our plans for another big exhibition in India. During the conversation, Master Han began to talk about

viii

PREFACE

the Cultural Revolution and gifted me this book *From Purgatory to Paradise* written by Mr Feng Jicai.

While coming back from the museum with Huang Qiang, I read the first chapter of the book on the subway and started crying. I became so emotional reading about the fate of Han Meilin during his early days and felt extremely sad. Sad, but determined to tell his story to the whole world. I got permission from both Han Meilin and Feng Jicai, and started working on it. Translating this book was not easy as Professor Feng writes in a very detailed, direct and charismatic manner, and the book is full of Chinese culturally-laden terms.

The great Indian translator Kumarajiva thinks that even the best translation is like chewed rice, tasteless and downright disgusting. However, I have tried to translate this book based on Nida's 'Functional equivalence theory'.

When I translated Mr Feng's works, I realised that translation is a matter of cross-cultural communication, like a wide spectrum beginning from the source language to the target language. To a certain extent, the loss of cultural significance in the translation process is indeed a pity, however, it is inevitable because no two cultures are equal. Therefore, if I lost some things that cover Chinese culture during the translation process and did not translate it into English properly; I can only seek your forgiveness, I can only be sorry, I can only apologise to Master Han and Professor Feng Jicai! I can only say, I'm sorry, as I am not qualified to be able to write the dialogues between two great people in English exactly the way Professor Feng has done.

PREFACE

Finally, I can say that translating Professor Feng's works was one of the greatest joys of my life. I hope to translate more of his works in the future and hope to translate his works not only into English but also into Hindi and Bengali. Hindi-speaking people are quite numerous in the world. About 550 million people speak Hindi and about 260 million read Bengali. Being able to let nearly two billion people (the number of people who speak English, Hindi and Bengali) understand Mr Feng's work will be the greatest joy of my life!

On 1 January 2020, I was in Beijing and went to meet Master Han Meilin again as I had many questions to put to him, and he spent around four hours explaining a slew of things which were not clear to me and helped me understand some of the phrases and sentences.

Apart from Master Han Meilin and Professor Feng Jicai, I must thank four other dear people. First and foremost, my son Yuvraj Kumar who encouraged me to translate this work. He showed genuine interest in my work and even read my translation. Second, to my Chinese brother Huang Qiang, who helped me understand some of the Chinese words and phrases. Mary Crosland helped immensely in proofreading and editing the work and finally my wife Taniya did not whine when I spent my evenings not with her but working on this book.

Last but not least, I would like to thank the publisher...

Yukteshwar Kumar

FOREWORD

I ONCE TOLD HAN MEILIN: "We've been lifelong friends but I've always owed you one thing — I've never written much about you and I must write a book on you".

The book I'm talking about won't be a general commentary. Although Han Meilin is a legendary person, it won't be a book of legendary tales. This book is an attempt to reveal his soul and is a book about the international art of a maverick. Han Meilin is like a mystery or even a miracle for many people and it's extremely difficult to understand his innerself and personality. Having said this, though, I reckon I know him extremely well— both the person himself and his art. Therefore, let me be responsible for introducing him to the outside world.

In my intermittent interaction with him over three decades, I've always tried to understand Han consciously or subconsciously. I've also tried to observe and understand him with my 'writer's hat' on, with calmness, inquisitiveness and professionalism. I solemnly admit, though, that

FOREWORD

despite knowing him for so many decades, I still feel that I don't understand him very well. What I mean is not his unlimited energy, inexhaustible artistic passion and inspiration, as well as him being an endless source of creativity— all these qualities come directly from heaven. It's impossible to research what is innate in nature.

What I mean rather is that he has experienced some strange phenomena— some completely unheard of and never divulged to the public. They include extreme humiliation and torture. We are two people from the same generation and I truly understand the meaning of the word 'torture'. I have also gone through very harsh tempering, but I am different from him. What I suffered was more of a mental torture whilst his included physical torture. He and Zhang Xianliang[1] experienced similar suffering, and what they suffered was fated as well as legendary.

However, I don't understand why the shadow of history is not mirrored in his paintings; there is no anger, hatred, bitterness or sadness. In his art, from the subject matter and image to the genre, emotion and colour, all is masculine, brilliant, pure and expansive. Everything is just pure, bright, colourful, and sunshine. Just like a vast ocean, even after experiencing stormy waves, he doesn't leave an iota of a shadow of suffering or anger. Is his soul full of only sunlight? He, of course, is a painter who paints from his soul. Why is his work like this? He avoids painting that unforgivable past. Either he's deliberately dodging it, or the shadow of those times never entered his heart. What kind of extraordinary relationship is there between his art and life? I can't figure it out.

xii

FOREWORD

This phenomenon is not unique to Han Meilin. In the West, a parallel example can be witnessed in the life of Vincent Van Gogh. I've visited the small town of Auvers-sur-Oise in the northwestern suburbs of Paris to see his last residence. In a dark hut less than eight square metres built on the top of the hill, one can still gauge the appalling condition of the place before his death. He often painted with no food in his belly, but the colours in his paintings are extremely beautiful and full of vitality and the charm of life.

One can find two kinds of painters in history. There are some like Bada Shanren and Edvard Munch who reflect the pain of their souls through the might of their brushes. Others are like Van Gogh and Han Meilin who, while bearing the darkness of their fate, turn their art towards brightness. Mozart was also like this—in the melody of sheer joy, he couldn't find any misfortune of his own.

I remember in the early 1980s after Han Meilin told me about his own predicament when meeting a pal – *Story of a Pup*–I wrote an essay entitled *Thank You, Life* with this theme and published it in the magazine *Chinese Writer* edited by Feng Mu.[2] This is one of my pieces which have been translated into several languages. I've read some comments on this essay at home and abroad and I regret to say that no one could understand it or was ready to try to explore the mystery of an artistic heart. On the contrary, they condemned me for praising the anti-human nature of Chinese society of that time. Why do we need to say "Thank You" for that kind of life?

FOREWORD

Han Meilin told me: "Real artists are indeed extraordinary people". They are the 'saints' of art. They use life to commemorate and celebrate beauty. Even during suffering, amidst various tribulations and ugliness, their minds look towards a bright future and what they pursue is only beauty. In one of the chapters of my autobiographical work *No Escape*, I dwelt upon some of the people I interacted with during the period of the Cultural Revolution. They were silent but passionately loved art. They longed for a beautiful future and lived a spiritually rich life in extremely poor conditions. I called this chapter *Waltz of the Artistic Life* but, of course, it was a deformed waltz. I believe in their way for I know and understand Han Meilin. However, in these times of marketisation an untainted artist of this kind is rare. I often feel touched that I have this kind of artist close to me.

In the essay *Thank You, Life*, my approach was that of writing a novel and expressing my perception of Han Meilin as an artist. But now what I want to do is to have a more in-depth discussion about the spiritual nature of this artist and to let him express himself directly in his own words. I want to use the method of David Dubal[3] in his work *Conversation with Menuhin* and conduct spiritual investigations through conversations and let Han express his soul directly through his own mouth. Oral conversations are first-hand, live, direct and personal. Only in this way can we confirm the existence of such an extraordinary artist, whilst allowing ourselves to progress through the sordid mechanisation and vulgar smoke, and find confidence in art.

Hence, I have separated the book into two parts. The first part is *Purgatory* while the second is named *Paradise*. The first part contains the experiences of Han Meilin and his own perception of them. This part is conversational autobiography, mainly his history of suffering. In *Paradise*, through the analysis of an artist's soul, we discuss the unique and sombre nature of Han Meilin's artistic world.

The main aim of the book is to figure out exactly how Han stepped out from the darkness of purgatory to the bright paradise of heaven.

Feng Jicai

For conciseness of the text and layout, the interviewer, Feng Jicai, is referred to as 'Feng' in the first instance and 'F' thereafter. The interviewee, Han Meilin, is referred to as 'Han' in the first instance and 'H' thereafter.

PART ONE
PURGATORY

Heated in three waters
Bathed in three bloods
Boiled in three lyes
Cleaner are we than clean.

ALEKSEY TOLSTOY
The Road to Calvary

Feng: I'm ready to start. I'm not writing your biography but your oral history so you must be prepared to talk. I know you're a legend in your own way: you were born in poverty and at the tender age of 13 you joined the army as a correspondent. Also, you were a child prodigy—in 1954 at the naïve age of 18, you had two educational books related to the Arts published by Shandong People's Publishing House. I've kept copies of them safe: *Basic Knowledge of Painting* and *Reference Painting Set for Teaching Drawing in Primary Schools*. However, my oral history of you begins with your 'getting trapped in misery'. I'd like you now to return to this 'misery'. I know that your suffering was like a purgatory and I know what it is like to be in purgatory ...

Two front cover pictures of fine art publications by Han during his teenage years (1954)

Han: No, that's wrong. How can you possibly know what it's like to be in purgatory? It was unrelenting, the uttermost part of purgatory — like the deepest eighteenth layer of hell in Buddhist mythology.

F: Then I'll have to be blunt. If you don't go back to the bad old days and answer my questions truthfully, then I can't reveal your heart.

H: I'm not scared. You can't be crueller than the Cultural Revolution. Come on, let's delve deep into purgatory

1

OVERTURE OF SUFFERING

1: MISFORTUNE EMANATING FROM THE MOUTH

F: Let us get straight into our conversation. When were you arrested? Were you arrested at the Central Academy of Arts and Design?

H: No, it was at Huainan Ceramic Factory in Anhui province. But my misery and misfortune started at the Central Academy of Arts and Design.

F: The root cause of misfortune for Zhang Xianliang was writing the poem *Great Wind Song*. When he wrote this poem, he was 17 years old. He was jailed five times and incarcerated for a total of 22 years. What about you? Why were you arrested?

H: For my speeches and opinions, for grumbling against the authorities.

F: Since the Anti-Rightist movement began in 1957 the tragedy for most intellectuals has been their 'speeches and

FROM PURGATORY TO PARADISE

opinions'. Were you a student or a teacher at the Central Academy at that time?

H: At the start, I was a student. In 1955, I was selected from Jinan to study at the Central Academy, and when the Central Arts and Crafts Institute was established the following year, I was selected for study there. My teachers were Pang Xunqin, Chai Fei and Zheng Ke, and Pang Xunqin was my mentor. They were all very famous teachers and artists in those days. Pang Xunqin especially was my revered teacher and mentor.

F: They were all outstanding artists and art educators. At that time, you were just a young student so when did you start making speeches challenging opinion? Was it during the Anti-Rightist Campaign instigated by Mao Zedong in 1957?

H: The Anti-Rightist Struggle was in full swing at the Academy. Many professors, including several of my teachers, were targeted. There were only 81 staff in the academy, but 18 were labelled 'rightists', including Pang Xunqin and Zheng Ke. Even Gao Zhuang, who designed the national emblem, was labelled as a rightist. I was very young and still a student and so allegations didn't matter much to me. Also, I came from a poor family and had joined the army at 13, so I was quite confident that I had demonstrated my loyalty towards the country and the revolution. In my mind, 'politics' was extremely simple— it was just 'communism'. How could I dream of uttering any reactionary word or getting involved in spying against my very own country? Far too mean an act! But, having said this, after the Anti-Rightist

OVERTURE OF SUFFERING

movement, many ideas started fluttering around in my head. Even if I didn't understand some things very well, I started talking about them. The fake dreams propagated in 'The Great Leap Forward'? I couldn't understand them at all! Sending all the intellectuals to labour camps? I didn't get it! As an outspoken person, I could never control my mouth and whatever I felt in my heart just came out. For example, when iron was being refined for steel, instead of the real production of steel, there was all this 'any old iron'[1]. Was I making it up? Another example: when we went to Baiyang lake for life drawing, the local peasants told us how some people had starved to death because of a famine and how the corpses had been taken by boat to other places. I'm not inventing this and why would the common people tell such a lie?

F: So, it was a bit absurd to convict you because of those words.

H: And there were a lot more absurdities. For example, in the debating class once, I and another student were asked to be in the opposition team while the rest of the class were in the proposition team. The topic was "the Americans making the bomb is not good for humanity". The opposition team was of course the 'enemy side' and we were forced to argue that "atom bombs are good" even though we didn't believe it. The proposers kept saying the Americans were evil and I just came out with: "If you say that we Americans are bad, we will send an atomic bomb to blow you up!" I didn't think even in my wildest dreams that these words which were uttered merely because I was playing a role, would later become a part of the allegation against me for making "reactionary remarks glorifying the US imperialists, and spreading hatred".

F: So, was it that simple to be 'crucified'? Didn't you have an opportunity to defend yourself?

H: Defend myself? Argue my case? Who with? I'm not sure whether you know but all these words were recorded in a file kept on me. There were so many incoherent and frightening things in that file. However, I didn't know about it then.

Photograph of a young Han in military uniform (12 April 1949)

F: This does seem to be rather frightening. You mean that there was always a note in the file about whatever you said or did? When did you discover this?

H: During the unfortunate time; during the period of the 'Socialist Education Movement' or the 'Four Clean-Ups'.[2] During the cleansing of politics, economics, ideology and organisation, everything which was hidden in the files was brought to public attention, and we were found 'guilty'. The Four Clean-Ups movement was a prelude to the 'Great Proletarian Cultural Revolution'. It was already extremely dangerous by then, if you were caught up in this then it would be extremely serious. For example, if you said that refining steel was basically recycling iron then you were accused of opposing the 'Three Red Banners'.[3] And who created the slogans of the Three Red Banners? Chairman

Mao! So, it was dubbed blatant opposition to Chairman Mao. You can imagine how serious the situation was. Ordinary little whispers created massive problems during those days of revolution.

Group photo with classmates on college graduation day in 1959

F: The Four Clean-Ups started in 1963 when you were 27. By that time, you'd graduated from the Central Academy of Arts and Design, hadn't you?

H: Yes, I graduated in 1959. After graduation, many of my paintings were published in newspapers and magazines and as I was recognised as an "exceptionally talented" student by the institute, I was appointed a faculty member in the Department of Fine Art and Design. However, after the Anti-Rightist movement of 1957, there was a huge increase in the

FROM PURGATORY TO PARADISE

reporting of and warning against so-called "problematic speeches and opinions" so that during my tenure as a teacher, I was the object of slander and abuse.

F: The disaster of the rightists in 1957 possibly came from careless talk. But there's something I don't understand. During the Anti-Rightist movement all your teachers were branded as rightists because of their so-called "problematic speeches and opinions". Why didn't you learn a lesson from them? Was it because you thought that as you were born in poverty and joined the army at a young age, your roots were 'red' and you couldn't be branded as a reactionary?

H: Perhaps, but I'm not sure. The main thing is that I haven't got a 'political head'. I'm not sensitive to politics; my mind is full of only painting and the arts. At that time, most of China's best painters and artists were all bunched up together in the Central Academy of Arts and Design and the Central Arts and Crafts Institute. Qi Baishi, Xu Beihong, Li Kuchan, Jiang Feng, Wu Zuoren, Jiang Zhaohe, Zhang Guangyu, Zheng Ke, Pang Xunqin, Ye Qianyu, Zhou Lingzhao, Huang Yongyu and many others. All of them were professors of high calibre and simply amazing, and several taught me. At that time, I was extremely energetic in my work. I just wanted to be a painter and I wanted to be a great painter. I didn't take a few complaints seriously. I only heard people say that I was professionally competent but not politically conscious, and my application to join the Youth League was repeatedly rejected, however I never heard people say that I was a reactionary.

OVERTURE OF SUFFERING

F: You are not sensitive to politics, but politics is not necessarily insensitive to you. Those engaged in art look at politics with an artistic vision and those who are engaged in politics, see artists from a political perspective. The judgment of politics is 'benefit' and 'harm' while the judgment of art is 'beauty' and 'ugliness'. So, when you say that some politics is 'ugly' then politics will look on you as 'harmful'. When did the problems begin?

H: As I just said, during the Four Cleans-Ups movement.

F: Was it at the Central Academy of Arts and Design?

H: No, in Anhui province.

F: How come in Anhui? Did you go there to get involved with the Four-Cleans-Ups movement? Or did you make a big mistake and were relegated and then taken to Anhui?

H: Your statement of 'being relegated' is along the right lines but not quite correct. In 1963 Anhui province wanted to establish an academy for art. The Provincial Party Committee Propaganda Minister Lai Shaoqi came to our college in Beijing to ask for support. He wanted a capable artist-teacher to help them set things up in Anhui for a maximum of three years. After that time, the teacher could return to Beijing. The authorities at the academy showed him one of my paintings and he was highly impressed and immediately wanted me to join them in Anhui. So, it was decided to send me there. I felt very proud and honoured but was completely unaware of the fact that they were using this as a pretext to kick me out of the Arts and Crafts Institute.

F: Was it because they wanted to blame you for the Freedom of Expression issue? Or was it just an excuse to send you into exile?

Photograph of Han as a teacher at the Central Academy of Fine Arts

H: Maybe. But I knew nothing about it. I'd just got married and eight days later, I went to the Light Industry Research Institute in Hefei, Anhui province, with my wife and three students. I was dreaming of doing a fantastic job there and helping make a glorious and prestigious Academy of Fine Arts and after completing my mission, of returning to Beijing as quickly as possible. At that time, I was doing exceedingly well in Beijing and people from all walks of life

OVERTURE OF SUFFERING

used to come to me requesting my paintings. Even Xia Yan, Fan Jin and Feng Mu wanted me to design covers for their books. The cover of Tian Han's play *The Injustice to Dou E* is one of my designs. I also remember that one time Deng Tuo saw one of my paintings and he immediately attached it to *Village Songs* – to the tune of Ta Sha Xing. I really wanted to go to Anhui quickly and then return as early as possible to enjoy and live in the rich culture of Beijing. The cultural ambience of that city is much richer than anywhere else. However, a year later, the art academy in Anhui province had not been established and the Four Clean-Ups movement had started, and I got caught up in that mess.

F: How?

H: Well, my files were in the archives of the Central Academy of Arts and Design. As soon as the Four Clean-Ups movement started, everything was made public. I was completely horrified when I heard about this: even the 'whisperings' and 'casual chats' of a normal day had been recorded. Who'd done this? As soon as I heard, it sent shivers down my spine. In normal circumstances these 'casual chats' wouldn't have been a problem but during the Clean-Ups every sentence could cause severe anxiety in body and soul. I suddenly realised that it was as though I was carrying a large box of my own hateful black records and had gone to Anhui to dig my own grave. Except it seemed that people had dug it beforehand, and then pushed me into it.

F: We shouldn't be surprised about this; it was pre-destined.

FROM PURGATORY TO PARADISE

"Village Songs" (painted by Han Meilin and inscribed by Deng Tuo), published in Beijing Evening News *on 22 July 1961*

2: TRAITOR

F: 'The Four Clean-Ups' movement caused a lot of trouble for you. Was there any other problem apart from the casual 'whispering'?

H: Yes, there was. But not in Beijing, in Anhui. It was very serious, a hundred times more serious than the Freedom of Speech issue, and it was a crime which could have led to the death penalty. But it was all made up, miles from the truth.

F: I don't get what you mean.

H: I'll have to tell you from two angles. One angle is Kong Yan and her boyfriend. Kong Yan was a female technician at our Light Industry Research Institute. She was a Shanghainese with a good temperament who liked the arts, and

OVERTURE OF SUFFERING

we would chat for hours. We became good friends. Her boyfriend, whose surname was Zhao, was engaged in atomic bomb research at the National Defence Science and Technology Commission. On his way to Shanghai with top secret material, he made a stopover at Hefei[4] to see Kong Yan. He decided on this without telling his office and getting prior permission. So, the man who was to meet him at the railway station in Shanghai waited in vain and then couldn't get hold of him at all. And Zhao was carrying confidential material! This was serious. So, although Zhao only stayed in Hefei for a day or two, because he hadn't told his office and had kept his visit secret, he was suspected of having leaked or sold confidential papers.

F: But what did this have to do with you?

H: Well, I'll now tell you the other part of the story. By coincidence, during those two days, I was in Shanghai to visit my mother and some other relatives. When I was at the Central Academy, I had a classmate named Sherek, who was from Poland. We shared a hobby of philately. I'd not seen him for many years. While in Shanghai, I went to buy some stamps in a stamp shop. I never expected to meet Sherek there, but I did, and it was good meeting up with an old classmate. He was working at the Polish Consulate in Shanghai, but I didn't know that. We strolled to a coffee shop but, unfortunately, we attracted the attention of the Security Department.

F: Yes, at that time society was quite closed. Foreigners were regarded as enemies and if you mixed with them, it was always considered sinister. If you became friendly with a

FROM PURGATORY TO PARADISE

blonde person then people became suspicious, and they kept an eye on you.

H: So, these were the two angles: on the one hand, a man carrying secret state information was untraceable; on the other, I appeared to be friendly with someone from the consulate of a foreign country. This caused distrust—not a trivial matter at all.

F: But these two angles were separate, weren't they?

H: No, both were related to Kong Yan and both happened in one city—Shanghai.

F: Did you meet Kong Yan's boyfriend?

H: I didn't know him at all. I've never seen him; I don't know what he looks like or even what his first name is. Anyway, be that as it may, there was an investigation at the Light Industry Research Institute. The National Defence Science and Technology Commission and the Ministry of Public Security came to investigate the 'missing or leaked secret documents' connected to Kong Yan's boyfriend and the Shanghai Security Department came to investigate the 'secret connections' between me and foreign embassies. Since I was Kong Yan's friend, they'd put two and two together. They alleged that Kong Yan's boyfriend gave me the top-secret material when he was 'untraceable' in Shanghai and then that, while enjoying coffee with Sherek, I secretly gave it to him to pass on to the Polish Embassy. It's a bit like a Hollywood spy movie, isn't it?

F: If it'd been true, it would have warranted the death penalty.

OVERTURE OF SUFFERING

H: Yeah: a secret agent selling major state secrets and committing treason!

F: But it was completely made up.

H: In those days facts and truth weren't needed at all. As soon as they suspected you, they started coercing you and forced you to admit the crime. The more you denied it, the fiercer they became and the greater the pressure.

F: But they had no proof.

H: Suspicion itself was the proof. During the Four Clean-Ups time, all my files had been deliberately altered. It was also alleged that while I was at the Academy of Fine Arts, I had a 'special' relationship with several other foreign students. One Iraqi, one Mongolian and yes, perhaps, there was a Bulgarian too. To be honest, all these foreigners had liked my paintings and I had a fantastic relationship with them. I didn't expect these relationships to be considered suspicious and to be included in my dossier.

F: It seems that in the dossier, you were certainly not a good person.

H: You may erroneously assume that you are loyal to your country; you may think that you are as pure as a blank sheet of paper, but in their eyes, you are a scribbled-on piece of paper, or even a completely black piece of paper. You aren't aware of this and you stupidly believe that people trust you.

F: So, they linked your relationship with those foreign students to this suspicion?

H: Why limit it to 'linking'? They all became extremely important clues for branding me a spy and leaking things to foreign countries. My relationships with every foreign student were thoroughly investigated.

F: Once again 'reactionary speech', once again 'revealing internal material to foreign countries'. I think the matter became extremely serious.

H: It was my supposed 'revealing of internal material to foreign countries' that was the major suspicion. The Ministry of Public Security, the Ministry of National Defence and the Anhui Public Security Bureau jointly filed a case for investigation. The Secretary of the Provincial Party Committee personally took an interest in investigated the matter and launched an extremely fierce tirade against me. I also came from Beijing, a big city, and that was taken very seriously. I became the main target for the entire Anhui Light Industry and the literary and art circles during the Four Clean-Ups. Whether you distastefully persecute me or kill me, I hated to be as abhorrent a person as Chiang Kai-shek.

F: When a movement starts, the main idea is to identify and punish as many people as possible. The more people are punished, the more successful the movement. At that time the government's success was not measured in terms of GDP, but in terms of the number of people punished. Were you scared?

H: Of course, I was — I'm not Superman. I was only in my twenties and had never got embroiled in politics. I'd never encountered or expected these kinds of problems and pres-

OVERTURE OF SUFFERING

sures which were strong enough even to push mountains down and create waves at sea.

F: What sort of pressures?

H: Trials. Trials like the ones held for convicts and criminals. You must admit everything according to their whims and fancies. How could I admit to all those baseless allegations? I'm a stubborn person; I wasn't going to confess. When I showed resistance, they started a struggle session[5]. They started pressurising me, one after another—further coercing and compelling. I'd never seen this kind of thing. And then many people started calling me names and started exposing me.

F: The people who were exposing you, what did they want to expose?

H: I hadn't committed any crime but they still wanted to expose me. A Shanghainese called Jiang alleged that the scar on his face was because of me pushing him from a building in 1939. Honestly! In 1939, I was only three years old! And at the time he was in Shanghai while I was in Jinan. These kinds of absolutely absurd and ridiculous lies were pinned on me during the meetings. People there used to shout slogans against me.

F: Why did Jiang want to expose you?

H: Well, he was born into a wealthy, capitalist family. During the class struggle, he was also suffering under huge pressure. He had to show his loyalty to the proletariat and so as soon as he got a chance, he pounced on me. But what I couldn't understand was that a student, whom I had

17

FROM PURGATORY TO PARADISE

brought from Beijing, also rebelled against me and exposed me. I'm still not very sure about his real motive, but he was born into a feudal landed family too. Generally, I'd treated him very well. Whenever I'd received some royalty money for my works or grain coupons[6], I used to put it under his pillow. I also used to talk with him about general subjects and discussed matters related to art in an open, frank and candid way. Of course, there were some things we disagreed about. I discussed with him some social issues and my concern about the problems in our society. On the first day of the struggle meeting, he stealthily told me not to worry and said: "I'm not going to complain about you". I hadn't expected that on only the second day, the first one to jump onto the stage and expose me would be him—my own student. His accusation was that once, when I saw a smiling picture of Chairman Mao waving his hand, I had commented that: "If Mao had known that there would be catastrophic deaths because of the 'Great Leap Forward', he wouldn't have been so happy". I had certainly said this. But at the time there were only the two of us in the room. If he hadn't revealed it to others, nobody would have known about it. His exposure rubbed salt into my wounds.

F: What you said was certainly perceived as a reactionary comment. I had a friend from Hunan province who was a teacher of language and literature. During the movement, the most lethal attacks in relation to exposures were made by the students who were very close to him. Those who knew him best caused the greatest damage.

H: The greatest damage to me was inflicted by my own wife. She revealed all our pillow talk to the authorities.

OVERTURE OF SUFFERING

F: You were truly beyond redemption.

H: I was in almost complete despair. A person like me, who was born into a poor family and who'd been in the army at a young age, a simple and innocent person, suffering from these tribulations felt like a kind of 'reward' from the revolution. My elder brother severed all ties with me and didn't allow his son to call me 'uncle', and when my wife stabbed me in the back and duped me, all my hopes were dashed. I had lost my family. I had had great ambition, I had wanted to become an excellent artist and to contribute something to society and to the country, but all my dreams evaporated. After the daily exposure and struggle sessions, the officials from the Public Security Department forced me into a dark room and checked the documents, asking me to plead guilty. Now I'd lost all hope. I wanted to die.

F: Did you ever try anything?

H: You mean suicide? Yes, I tried. Once, in the lavatory, I saw a pile of lime on the ground—dirty and smelly with lots of ants and bugs crawling on it. I grabbed and swallowed a lot of it. I wanted to burn myself with the lime. However, I didn't realise that if lime stays in the open for a long time, it deteriorates. It won't burn. On the contrary, as it contains calcium, it gave me the calcium which my body lacked. I didn't die, but my ambition was thoroughly dead. Do you know what it's like to kill a person's ambition?

F: If I look at it from a social angle, I've also tasted it. But of course, not with as much cruelty as you endured. What happened regarding the accusations?

FROM PURGATORY TO PARADISE

H: There was no basis or proof of 'smuggling internal matters to a foreign country'. Even the gossip that I had met Kong Yan's boyfriend was baseless and couldn't be verified. In the end, they stopped talking about it. I heard that Kong Yan's boyfriend was transferred from his office and so was Kong Yan herself. However, I couldn't escape the accusation of being highly opinionated. In the end, I was labelled as an 'internal counter-revolutionary'. The people were to decide what was to happen. I was to be sent to the Huainan Ceramic Factory to undergo 'reform through labour'.

F: What year was that?

H: May 1964. After a struggle session in Hefei, I was sent straight to Huainan.

3: NINE REGIONS, EIGHTEEN POSTS

F: Where is Huainan Ceramic Factory?

H: The Huainan Ceramic Factory is in the north of Hefei city near Bagong mountain at Huainan. It's a very desolate and wild place with almost no cultivation at all and in the past was called "the city where dogs pee". Huainan is widely spread out. In the beginning people started mining here. Wherever a mine was found, people would settle but they were not inter-connected so there were nine railway stations, one in each of the nine districts. It is commonly known as the "nine districts and eighteen posts". Bagong mountain is not very tall or grandiose but is quite famous. The idiom "when in extreme panic, people become oversuspicious" originated here and you can check this in the book

Comprehensive Mirror in Aid of Governance[7]. The people there weren't civilised, and were quite fierce and violent. In the past it was bandit-ridden and there is a local saying that "In nine districts and eighteen posts, each post produced one bandit". The ceramic factory was based in the earthen dam area of Caijia post.

The damaged wall of Huainan Ancient Town, which no longer exists today

F: Was it a small factory?

H: No, it was an enormous place with around 2,000 people.

F: What did such a large porcelain factory produce?

H: It mainly produced large ceramic bowls. The bowls used in the rural areas in the nearby provinces were all made there so there was a lot of production.

F: Were they that kind of rough ceramic blue and white bowl?

FROM PURGATORY TO PARADISE

H: They were even thicker than those. The flowers on the top were not hand-painted but sprayed. There was a song for these kinds of bowls:

"While eating, wear a mask;
While washing, wear a glove;
If put inside the house, rats might nibble;
If put outside in the garden, the sparrows will dribble".

Why would rats and sparrows be attracted and nibble? Because the pores on the stoneware bowls were quite big— big like an eye hole, the rice husks remain there, and the rats and sparrows naturally get attracted to these.

F: What did you do at the ceramic factory? Most people spray decorations. What could you do about your painting?

H: Painting? Are you mad? I was the chief object of reform through labour[8], and I was given the roughest, hardest, most painful and most difficult jobs to do. I was assigned to the third workshop. There were five people in this workshop —I was the only male; the rest were females. The females did clay casting and sprinkled water on the flowers. I was asked to do the heavy work including transporting materials, handling them and putting the pots into the kiln. At the time of firing, around thirty clay bowls were put on a very long board, weighing about thirty kilos. One after another, these heavy boards had to be inserted into the kiln. After all the boards were inside, I had to stand in front of the kiln and kept feeding fuel into it. The temperature of this type of kiln reached around 1200 degrees centigrade and the temperature in the workshop would reach about five degrees. During

OVERTURE OF SUFFERING

the summer you could only frantically drink water. This was freely available. I myself felt that I was like a clay bowl and wished I could also be fired in a kiln so that I wouldn't have to suffer any more of those miserable days.

F: Was it really that bad?

H: It was not a human life. It was like the life of animals— after working hard all day, we would sleep and after a little sleep, work again. Nobody gave a damn about me. I was an anti-revolutionary—who would care for me? Everybody used to keep a close eye on me.

F: Did your wife go to the ceramic factory with you?

H: She'd already drawn a line under our marriage and left. Do you really think she would have come with me to the reform through labour camp? She was herself engaged in exposing me and because this was quite successful, she was sent to Bengbu[9] to take part in the Four-Clean Ups movement with my former student who had also exposed me. In the first year of our marriage, after we had come from Beijing to Anhui, she had given birth to a daughter. I was missing my daughter, so one day I managed to escape to Bengbu with a plan to meet them both. But I met ....

F: Is this uncomfortable for you?

H: No, I'm all right .... I was humiliated. After arriving in Bengbu, I learnt that she'd gone to watch a movie. I immediately rushed to the cinema. After the movie was over, I was surprised to see her coming out with that student who had tried to expose me. As soon as I saw that they were holding hands and seemed quite close, I understood everything.

FROM PURGATORY TO PARADISE

Despite this, I went up to her and asked how she and our daughter were. At that time, I was in rags. People don't look decent in misery and misfortune. She looked at me as if I was a beggar asking for money. She looked over me in such a cold and disdainful way. You can imagine if someone gets humiliated by society and on top of that, gets this kind of emotional betrayal, what they feel like. I'm a man. I haven't hurt anybody in my life. I'm a moral person and you can understand my feelings at that time.

F: We can talk about this when you are calmer. Now I would like to know whether during this period you met anybody who was sympathetic to you, even if only slightly. My own experience tells me that when one is in big trouble, there is always somebody to give human warmth and support. This is probably what we say is a "Blessing of the Almighty". Even if it is only a little bit, it gives huge support during a desperate situation.

H: Yes, I had someone.

F: Who was this kind soul?

H: A dog.

F: Is this the famous *Friend in Adversity* [10]? What kind of dog was it?

H: I was working hard every single day and just managing to survive. Nobody cared for me. While eating, I used to sit alone under a willow tree because everyone else used to sit far away from me. And there was this dog which was attracted to me, and he used to come up to me and give me a friendly stare. He was the family pet of a manager of the

OVERTURE OF SUFFERING

factory, whose name was Yang. I wasn't sure if he was hungry or not so I would just put a piece of meat, vegetables, a slice of loaf from my bowl on the ground or throw a small piece of steamed bread to him, and gradually we became friends. He was ugly, dark brown with black spots, and nobody cared about him. He would often come to me wagging his tail and he liked to play with me. Even though the place where I was working was extremely hot, he would still come running to me and wasn't afraid of the heat of the kiln. Sometimes there were sparks but he didn't care. He'd always come looking for me and, though he couldn't understand me, I'd speak a few words to him.

F: Did you still complain? Did you open your heart and talk about wicked things and unsatisfactory matters?

H: Even if I grumbled, he wouldn't expose me. In the whole world, this dog was the only being that wasn't going to expose me. You can't imagine how I felt when the only one who became my friend and to whom I dared to confide everything, turned out to be a dog.

F: This was your good fortune and at the same time also a misfortune for the whole of society.

H: At that time, I certainly felt that I was fortunate.

F: What did you call him?

H: Son.

F: Oh! Did you really call him 'Son'?

H: Oh, Yes! I just named him 'Son'.

25

FROM PURGATORY TO PARADISE

F: You make me feel your great affection for the dog which was higher than your love for humans. It also reminds me of the words of the writer Zhou Keqin[11]: "The son is always faithful".

H: Let me tell you about another incident. I'd been working in the Huainan Ceramic Factory for more than a year. I was considered a very honest person. I was a painter and the flower designs that I designed and sprayed on the pots were much better than the others. Therefore, I gradually became the authority on spray technology in the workshop. The manager of the workshop started trusting me and once sent me out to buy something. I took this opportunity and went to the train station to catch a train. I told you earlier that there were nine stations in the city. You had to catch a train to go from one side of the city to the other. When I got into the train compartment, Son came running and grabbed my clothes. He tried to drag me away with all his strength. I told him that I had to go to work but would return in the evening. But he wouldn't listen to me. Anyhow, I managed to get rid of him, but he started chasing after the carriage where I was, but he couldn't catch up with the train. While I was watching him chasing the train without stopping, I felt a different kind of emotion in my heart. What kind of affection was it, do you think?

F: The highest level of affection is pure feeling. God is fair. When the world and your own family betrayed your love, this dog gave you the most pure and disinterested affection. You lost your daughter; Almighty God gave you a son.

H: Yes, you're right.

OVERTURE OF SUFFERING

F: Were you still painting?

H: Yes, of course.

F: Was it not the case that all your ambitions and aspirations for painting were already destroyed?

H: I couldn't restrain myself; perhaps I'm an instinctive painter.

F: As I said earlier, they were ruining your ambitions in a social sense but in art and your basic instincts—the ambition and aspiration for creating fantastic paintings—they still existed. This was the most important thing.

H: Yes, no one should have dreamt that they could destroy my basic instinct for painting. God sent me into this world to paint.

F: What you are talking about is the basic instinct of an artist. That's why art cannot be inherited through blood relationships. This basic instinct only belongs to true artists.

H: But some people want to change the artist's innate nature and want them to draw according to their whims and fancies.

F: Then they must be careful to keep themselves intact. Being distorted may be worse than being destroyed. What did you paint in this period?

H: I painted whatever came into my heart and mind: beautiful images, even some people's ugly faces, and various ideas, compositions, designs, sketches. Everything.

F: What materials did you use?

H: Paper picked up from anywhere and homemade brushes, some made of fallen dog hairs. I compiled a book of these paintings and wrote two words on the cover: *Compiling Footsteps*.

F: Why did give you this name: *Compiling Footsteps?*

H: So as to say that I was leaving my footprints in my art.

F: Judging by this name, one could gauge that you had an explicit idea about your artistic adventures even in that situation.

H: The fate of *Compiling Footsteps* is very strange. There was a worker in our factory called Xiao Pan. He also liked to paint, and he borrowed the book from me. During the Cultural Revolution, when I was arrested and imprisoned, he dismembered the whole book and hid all the pictures behind the frame of a mirror in his home. When I was released, he reassembled it and gave it back to me.

F: Were you arrested at the start of the Cultural Revolution?

H: Not immediately. Huainan, where I was based, is in a peripheral region unlike central cities like Beijing, Tianjin and Shanghai. At the beginning of the Cultural Revolution, our factory was in complete chaos and the workers united and rebelled. Nobody was in charge. I was often asked by the rebels to write big-character posters[12]. Nobody could write Chinese characters more attractively than me, you see. Whatever they ordered me to write, I would write. At that time many intellectuals were rehabilitating[13] themselves and it crossed my mind that I should do the same. I thought of Cai Xiaoli, a former classmate at the Central Academy of

OVERTURE OF SUFFERING

Arts and Design. She was a very decent human being—kind and compassionate. I knew her very well. She was in Hangzhou. I thought I would find her and get her to write a testimonial to prove that I was a good person.

F: That was a very naïve idea.

H: Well, I've never been mature, and I don't want to be! Nobody in the office was bothered so I just bought a train ticket and went to Hangzhou to look for Cai Xiaoli and pour my heart out to her. But she was in a quandary as she didn't know what to write or who to write to. After a bit of thought, I realised that I hadn't planned very well: I didn't know what I should ask Cai Xiaoli to write, how to phrase it and who to send it to. So, I would have to think of something else. In Hangzhou I witnessed a really shocking event: the exposing of Gai Jiaotian[14].I loved watching Beijing opera and Gai Jiaotian was like a god to me. At that time, they were burning his colourful costumes in the street and smoke was billowing in the sky. Gai Jiaotian was over eighty then, and he couldn't bear it. He was ordered to sit in a reclining chair, which he did, looking at the sky as though he was in a stupor. His mouth was wide open, and his head was half-shaved. He looked like a half human-half ghost, a long way from the character of Wu Song which I remembered so well. A group of rebellious Red Guards was shouting slogans against him. The streets were full of people and houses were getting raided. If such a giant figure was made to suffer like this, then the world was certainly in pandemonium. Thinking about myself, I didn't know what fate was waiting for me in the future.

Huainan City in the 1970s

4: 7 APRIL 1967

F: I've done a bit of research on you and I think that what you've just told me is like the trailer for a movie. Your real suffering started from the Cultural Revolution, right? Do you remember when it started?

H: 7 April 1967.

F: How can you remember the precise date?

H: If you'd had to suffer, you'd also not forget it for as long as you lived. That day is like a knife stabbing me in the back.

F: It wasn't long after you returned from Hangzhou, was it?

H: I was sent a letter and was completely petrified. I felt that something ominous was going to occur and I was literally trembling with fear. When I went to Hangzhou, I made a

OVERTURE OF SUFFERING

special trip to Shanghai to see my mother. At that time, my sister-in-law was working at a hospital. I told her I couldn't sleep properly, and could I get some sleeping pills. I asked for these several times and managed to get dozens of them. My plan was that if there was a really, really bad time, I would swallow a lot of them to commit suicide. I'll tell you about that later. Anyway, when I returned to the factory, I learnt that many people who had caused 'problems' in the past were now going to be persecuted and harassed. Even the chief manager of the factory, Dai Yue, had been targeted. After a few days I went to a department store in Caijia post with a technician to buy some necessary stuff. On the way back, when I was carving a piece of wood and making a small human bust as I walked along, one of my colleagues, Zhu, who had been quite active during the Four Clean-Ups movement, cycled up to me and said: "There is an urgent matter at the factory, and you need to go back there immediately". I turned back and Zhu followed me, keeping an eye on me. I felt that something was wrong.

I was about eighty metres from the factory gate when I saw a very large group of people. They were waiting for me at the gate like a cartload of monkeys. When I arrived, they all stared at me. As soon as I saw them, I knew there was trouble coming.

F: Can you give more details?

H: I subconsciously put the woodcarving and the knife in my pocket. Then people started coming towards me with thick sticks in their hands, hurling abuse—and then one of them kicked me. I fell down in pain and curled up on the

31

FROM PURGATORY TO PARADISE

ground. They tied both my hands and arms with wire. They were constantly kicking and hitting me, and they took me to the first floor of the office building. As soon as I was dragged there, a tall, lanky, cocky man named Wu, who was notorious in the factory for being a bully, slapped me in the face and I rolled down the stairs to the ground floor. He picked me up, turned left and then right, and took me to the Security Office. With one foot he made me kneel on the ground, while with a heavy stick in his hand he pressed my feet and yelled: "Confess to your crimes!" At that moment, I saw that the head of the Security Department, a military representative, and the chief of the Worker's Propaganda Team were there. I knew disaster was on the way.

F: Were you very frightened?

H: To tell the truth, yes at first, I was scared, but later I wasn't. I had to face all these people, so I knew it was useless getting scared. To be honest, I didn't even know that I should be scared. I knew in my heart that whatever opinions I'd stated, I'd already confessed and explained them. I wasn't a KMT[15] spy and I hadn't done anything terribly bad in my life. What else had I to explain? If there was a dictatorship, then let there be a dictatorship. I would fight it. I said: "I've already explained everything." There was a man whose surname was similar to yours. He came forward and forcefully jumped on the thick stick which was already on my leg. Earlier, I had read about how the Japanese devils used to trample on the feet of captured Eighth Route army personnel and guerrillas, using thick sticks. However, I only really learned what it was like after it happened to me. My whole body was cold—I can't explain it now, and it hurt

OVERTURE OF SUFFERING

terribly—my heart sank. I was also sweating profusely. This bloke then said: "You've got a real hard mouth on you, let me repair it for you." Then he twisted the heavy wooden stick and crushed my legs. It was excruciating. All the bones of my feet were broken.

F: How did you know that bones were broken?

H: I had an X-ray later and found out that six bones had been broken into more than forty pieces. In this agonising pain I shouted: "Fuck your mother!" Although I wanted to shout a lot more, I couldn't because my mouth was full of blood. They asked: "What's your relationship with the writers of *Sketches of a Three-Family Village?* [16] What's your connection with the Four Reactionary Writers?[17] How about your association with Deng Tuo? You paint pictures for them; you are hand in glove with them." Now I realised that the Beijing Central Arts and Crafts Institute had transferred to the factory a batch of 'new materials' related to me. I didn't think that knowing Tian Han, Xia Yan or Deng Tuo was a crime. Were they not giant writers and artists? Who knew that they would become the biggest enemy and would be mentioned daily in the newspapers and on big posters? Whatever sins I may have committed in a previous existence, I was paying back in this life for being a counter-revolutionary!

F: This was your fate but only people of our generation can have this kind of fate. Your name was linked with great writers like Deng Tuo and Tian Han. What can be worse than that? You were doomed.

FROM PURGATORY TO PARADISE

H: At that time, I also thought I couldn't escape my fate. I viewed death as "returning to my own home". I steeled my heart and murmured: "I don't have anything to explain." That man Feng suddenly took a fruit knife out of the paint brush holder on the desk, brandished it, grabbed my hand, plunged it into the muscle in my wrist and pulled it out again. Baring his teeth, he ordered: "I'll teach you how to paint, and you'll paint!" The red, tender muscles of my wrist became visible, and blood rushed out. Surprisingly I didn't feel any pain. The only thought that came into my mind was that perhaps I wouldn't be able to paint anymore, that my ideals, my ambitions, and my interests were all gone, and he had ruined my career. I once again yelled at him: "Fuck your mother!"

I was totally desperate. They were still trying to press my leg with the wooden bar but their efforts were unsuccessful. Then they burnt me with cigarette butts and tied wire around my arm. See. Look at my hand just above my thumb: this is the place where they broke my bones; this is the scar where they burnt me. They're still here, permanent marks.

F: Do you want to take a rest? Let us stop.

H: No, I'll carry on. I was born brave. I've never been faint-hearted. At that time, since I wasn't afraid of anyone, I became more valiant, intrepid and audacious. If somebody beats you, the more terrified you get and if you give in, the more you will get bullied. Somebody told me that because I was a very brave man, the severity of torture was worse for me than for other people. That may be true, however, that's my nature too—how can I change it?

OVERTURE OF SUFFERING

I'll continue the story. After brutally beating me, they took me onto the street for a shame parade[18] in front of the public. In the factory, people were gathering in huge numbers, and they started beating drums, shouting slogans and singing revolutionary songs. In the courtyard of the factory, there was another group of people who were targets of attacks and were ordered to put on dunces' caps and be placed on a pedestal. The factory manager and the Party Secretary of the factory were also there, as was an accountant who had been a member of the 'Three Green Group'[19] during their high-school years. Now he was labelled as an "historical counter-revolutionary". This accountant was suffocated in a pile of lime. I saw it myself.

They took the wooden bar away from my leg, but I couldn't stand up on my own. It seemed that my legs didn't belong to me. They took me downstairs and the parade of humiliation started. It went from the east gate of the factory, around a large round-about and then re-entered the factory from the west gate. The whole street was full of people watching and they threw stones, plaster, mud, coal and anything else they could find. Some slapped my face. My whole body was covered in shit and my nose was bleeding. I didn't look like a human being.

My legs felt like wood, the bones in both my feet were smashed, and my broken leather shoes were full of blood. My feet were so swollen that I couldn't walk. I took off my shoes and carried them. I don't know how my legs survived for so long. What gave me strength was not people pushing and shoving me, but two old peasants and two children walking in front of me.

F: What were they doing there?

H: There were several shame parades on the streets at the same time. When they met, they used to get mixed up with each other. Those peasants and children came from other parades and walked in front of us. Of the two peasants, one sold cabbage and the other bought cabbage. At that time when peasants bought and sold their own agricultural products, they were branded as "treading on the path of capitalism". It was a coincidence that they were arrested and dragged into the street together. They each had a gong in their hand and the peasant who had sold cabbage was in the front. While banging his gong, he had to shout: "I should not have sold cabbage." The peasant who had bought cabbage banged on his gong and said: "I should not have bought cabbage." The two children were primary school pupils from a local village. The school had ordered the pupils to pick up scrap iron lying outside the school. There was a minimum amount that each pupil had to collect. Sometimes the children couldn't find any iron, so they went to the factory and stole it from there. Each of these children had stolen an iron bar but had unfortunately been caught by the factory workers and then pushed into the street's shame parade. The two children were ordered to carry the stolen iron bar which weighed more than nine kilos. They'd already walked quite far carrying it. They couldn't bear the weight and were bent over like hooks, but they carried on walking. The image of the two children gave me strength. If they could walk, why couldn't I? Everywhere I walked, I left bloody footprints.

F: I can't even envisage how you were feeling at that time.

OVERTURE OF SUFFERING

H: But then a miracle happened, and my 'son' suddenly appeared.

F: Your son? Oh, your dog? Where did he come from?

H: He suddenly sprang out of the crowd and threw himself at me. Two front paws hugged me warmly, pulled my clothes, got into my crotch, sniffed my knees, smelt my legs...as if he didn't know what to do, as if he knew I was suffering. I was covered with dirt and blood and didn't look human, so how did he recognise me? But the men who were humiliating me wanted to scare him away and they shouted at him. However, Son was not going to budge, let alone leave. They were furious and started swinging massive wooden sticks at him. Son screamed. Several sticks hit him on the back, and I guess they broke his spine. Eventually he ran off out of the crowd, but the fact that he'd been there gave me strength.

F: How?

H: Emotion is power. Showing humanity is also strength.

F: Unfortunately, that humanity was not shown by humans. It was left to a dog. Was his spine really broken?

H: I didn't see him again that day.

F: Did you know that Ba Jin[20] was so moved by the story of your dog that it reminded him of what happened to his dog and led him to write his famous *Story of a Pup*?

H: Yes, I know.

F: Did you hear anything about 'your son' afterwards?

FROM PURGATORY TO PARADISE

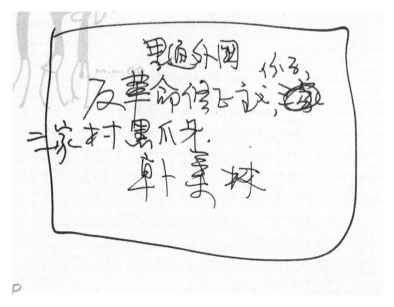

A sketch (by Han Meilin) of the sign hung around prisoners' necks during struggle sessions

H: I did, but let's talk about him later.

F: At that time, I believe you weren't doing any painting?

H: You may not believe me but exactly at that time I was working on a painting.

F: It seems hardly possible. Was it from your imagination?

H: No, it was a painting from real life. When we returned from the shame parade, we—the so called 'evil monsters' stood on the front steps of the auditorium and waited for dinner. After dinner, we were going to be paraded again in the street. Suddenly I realised that my leather shoes which I had been carrying were full of blood. I also noticed that blood from the toe of my shoe was dripping on the ground and the shape resembled a chicken's head. I felt like painting

OVERTURE OF SUFFERING

and so I drew a chicken with the toe of my shoe dipped in blood.

F: In that perilous situation, how could you draw and do it with blood? Where did the instinct come from?

H: Perhaps an inherent, natural instinct and, as I said earlier: "Because I was born to draw and paint."

F: The reality was so cruel, simply unfathomable. Incredible!

H: Art comes naturally to me.

F: What did the chicken look like?

H: It was a rooster standing on its feet, perhaps like this. [*Makes a gesture*].

F: Was it beautiful?

H: Of course, it was beautiful. It was drawn from my heart and had no relationship with my stressful reality.

F: It may have been beautiful, but it was drawn with blood. If it still existed, then it would be the greatest painting of the Cultural Revolution. It would be no less great and significant than Pablo Picasso's famous *Dove of Peace*. However, we don't have the work.

H: While I was drawing this 'Chicken from Blood', a bunch of twelve or thirteen-year-old teenagers came up to us so-called 'evil monsters', hit us with peeled willow twigs and ordered us to call them "Daddy". They also kicked us. We were battered already; how could we survive a kicking from these kids?

39

F: What did you do?

H: The kids were clearly not aware what they were doing. They were just indulging in mischief. Besides, you can't blame them. It was society that made them believe we were the bad elements. We had no option but to call them "Daddy". We continuously called them "Daddy... Daddy".

F: Did the humiliation parade continue in the afternoon?

H: Yes, we were paraded for almost five miles that day. I don't know how my two broken feet managed such a long distance. After the parade ended, we were sent to the detention centre of the Public Security Bureau. When I entered the building, a guard came up, kicked my knees and shouted: "I now order the counter-revolutionary of the Huainan Ceramic Factory, Han Meilin, who has been detained, to come here and sign". After I signed, the factory workers walked away, and I was left at the mercy of the police. A police officer undid the wire that tied my hands and feet. My hands, feet and body were either purple or black. Then two policemen escorted me through the yard and took me into a room.

On entering the centre, you had to register and then hand over all your belongings. I took off my belt and handed it over, along with my identity card, some money, and the wood carving. The knife had fallen out on the street during the humiliation parade. I didn't know how many days or years I would be detained there. When I was released my belt was completely rotten because it had been stained with blood and sweat.

OVERTURE OF SUFFERING

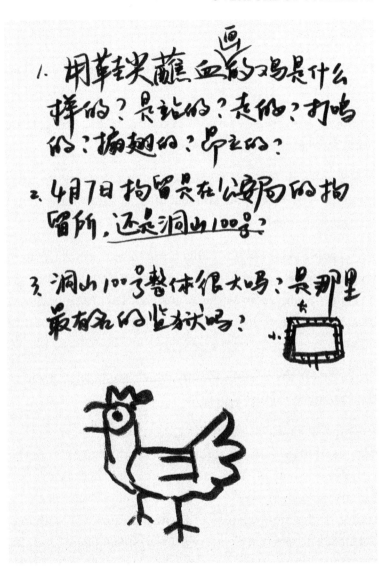

"Chicken from Blood" by Han Meilin

5: NINE DAYS

F: How long were you in the detention centre?

H: Nine days.

F: What did you do during that time? Were you interrogated?

H: Nobody interrogated me, but I continued to be repeatedly humiliated at the struggle sessions.

F: Weren't you under the supervision of the Public Security Bureau? Why were you still being dragged out to attend struggle sessions?

H: I hadn't yet been formally arrested and anyway, there was complete anarchy in there. Whoever wanted to do anything could do so without any problem. Besides, I was like meat on a chopping board; anyone could cut a slice of me.

F: Was it still the ceramic factory which was dragging you to the struggle sessions?

H: Sometimes it was the factory. At other times some other organisations would come for me. I was the superstar of the struggle sessions of Huainan city. I was labelled as a "reactionary speech maker", "a spy for foreign countries", "a traitor to the motherland" and "the gangster who colluded with the authors of *Sketches of a Three-family Village* and the Four Reactionary Writers". Was there anybody in Huainan who was more reactionary than me? Was there anybody else who could be linked with the authors of *Sketches of a Three-family Village* and the Four Reactionary Writers? I had had something to do with all of them including Deng Tuo, Tian Han, and Xia Yan. Ferreting out a man like me was a commendable job, wasn't it? How satisfying it must have been to drag me into the struggle sessions! In theatres, people like to listen to famous actors! Later I was taken to struggle sessions in Hefei also. It was like the promotional tours that famous stars go on these days. But the most humiliating struggle sessions were at the ceramic factory.

F: Oh my God! So cruel!

H: They used most cruel methods to 'rectify' us. They made us kneel down separately in front of the main gate.

F: Were there many spectators and was it in full public glare?

H: Oh, yes and then they told everyone to spit on us.

F: Did they?

H: Oh yes. People vomited, spat, rubbed snot on us. Our faces and bodies were covered with stinking stuff. Sticky and thick. It started running down us. My whole body was like a runny nose. It took just one day for you to become covered with shit.

F: Even those who knew you spat on you?

H: You see, spitting or not spitting was an attitude towards the enemy of class-based hierarchy. I, Han Meilin, had fallen and all began to tread on me. However, there were some moral souls there. They would just turn their heads and pretend not to see me. There was a female colleague who used to work with me in the same division and she would deliberately turn her face away and start talking to somebody else pretending that she didn't see me 'genuflecting' there. Then there was a girl called Huang who had gradu-

FROM PURGATORY TO PARADISE

ated from the Ceramic School. I didn't know her very well but not only did she not spit, but she also nodded to me with a cheesy grin. These kind gestures will remain with me forever.

F: Although common people weren't the initiators of the Cultural Revolution, everyone participated in it according to their own nature and morals.

H: During the struggle sessions the rebels wrote a lot of derogatory terms about me on a heavy plaster of Paris plaque. These included "counter-revolutionary revisionist", "lackey of the writers of *Sketches of a Three-family Village*", "Han Meilin, traitor and spy, who divulged confidential information to enemy countries". My name was also crossed out with red ink. This plaque was tied round my neck with wire. It was incredibly heavy, and the wire kept digging into my skin. The bones of my feet were still broken, and I couldn't stand properly. If I became unsteady, they said that I was being dishonest. A rebel came and abused me and said he would smash my face in. He came with a heavy stick and hit the plaque and broke it into pieces. After that he made a plaque out of paper, rewrote all the humiliating words on it and hung it round my neck. This paper plaque was much lighter, so I was more comfortable. His name was Fang and he had come from Zibo to join us in the ceramic team. I realised he had deliberately smashed the heavy plaster and put a lighter one on me. The clever man had had a deliberate plan to help me.

F: In a similar fashion I saved an old woman in my neighbourhood. When the Red Guard tried to set fire to her, I

OVERTURE OF SUFFERING

poured a bucket of water over her head, saying she should "wash away her sins". Actually, I extinguished the fire. I wrote about this in my memoirs of the Cultural Revolution called *No Road to Escape*. At that time, there were few heroes like Zhang Zhixin[21] who stood firm against the Cultural Revolution. Generally, people with conscience had only two ways to deal with it. One was to keep silent because of everything that was happening. The other was to resist in a clever way. That was the harsh reality of the Cultural Revolution because of the tyranny. I wrote this in the book *Ten Years of a Hundred People*[22]: "The success of any ruler lies in the exploitation of the weakness of the ruled". We were exploited by feudal society for thousands of years. But your story tells us that after darkness there is light. Now our hope is that human feeling has not completely perished.

H: Two of the struggle sessions left a strong impression on me. One was an art troupe in Huainan. That session was quite special. The art troupe was full of young and beautiful actors and actresses, shouting loud, crisp slogans in powerful voices. They were reading the critique much like reciting a poem. Their attitude towards me was also not very fierce. When my so-called "Black Paintings" were exhibited, unexpectedly some people appreciated them. There were some artists in the art troupe. I heard them comment: "This is a very good painting." I was a senior and talented student of the Central Academy of Arts and Crafts. It was very difficult to see pictures of that standard in such a remote area as Huainan.

45

FROM PURGATORY TO PARADISE

F: But wasn't your house wrecked during the Socialist Education Movement? How come there are still some paintings?

H: Since the time of the Four Clean-Ups, my house had been wrecked seven or eight times. Of course, there weren't any paintings. So as to give the people a stick to beat me with, they had been temporarily borrowed from the Provincial Public Security Bureau and the Light Industry Centre. The Public Security Department didn't understand the paintings. They thought that all my paintings were "Black Paintings" and if they displayed them, then I and my paintings would be criticised and condemned. However, they were all beautiful decorative paintings so displaying them was equivalent to holding a free exhibition for me.

At noon, a beautiful actress brought me a bowl of noodles and even put some juicy meat into it. When I returned to the detention centre, I felt something in my pocket. When I looked, I found ten yuan and a food coupon that was worth ten kilos of grain. It must have been the actress who had secretly stuffed them into my pocket. If all the struggle sessions could have been like that, how wonderful it would have been. I really wanted the Huainan Cultural Art Corps to get me to go there again for another session.

F: You said that two sessions were very special. What was the other one?

H: It was conducted by the Huainan Literary and Art Circles. The atmosphere was completely different and very tense. Among the six people in the session was the director of the Huainan Cultural Bureau. I was like a pundit among the reactionaries because I'd come from Beijing. At the session a young lad was especially active and after loudly reading "a supreme instruction"[23] from the higher authorities; he led the whole audience in shouting slogans. Perhaps he was stressed because he became very nervous and instead of shouting "Down with Liu Shaoqi!" he made a mistake and shouted: "Down with Chairman Mao!" There was chaos in the audience. He was immediately pushed onto the stage with his hands tied behind his back. A brand-new counter-revolutionary had been born! Basically, he'd got himself into this mess.

I'll tell you an even more bizarre story. An old leader who was presiding over a struggle session was also very nervous. The more afraid he was of making mistakes, the more mistakes he made. In the end, instead of saying: "Don't forget the class struggle", he said loudly: "No class struggle at all". When he realised that he had reversed his words and made a huge gaffe, he became extremely anxious and started crying and then slapped his own face. Another counter-revolutionary had been born!

I stood on the stage with my head bent and wondered how two such interesting dramas could have appeared in a row. Even Shakespeare wouldn't have been able to write such a thing. I chuckled and was seen smiling by some people. He shouted: "See, Han Meilin laughed just now!" Of course, this drama did not prevent me getting fewer slaps and this kind of bizarre session was very rare.

F: Can I ask what happened after the nine consecutive days of struggle sessions?

FROM PURGATORY TO PARADISE

H: The session on the ninth day was held in front of the detention centre. At the end of it, I was officially charged and arrested for my 'counter-revolutionary crimes'. That day was like a line between the everyday world and purgatory. What I'd suffered before was human suffering. From that day I began to suffer the hardships of purgatory.

2
HISTORY OF PURGATORY

1: NO. 100, DONGSHAN

F: When were you arrested?

H: 8 May 1967. I'll never forget that day. I officially became a member of purgatory.

F: Where were you imprisoned? Did you stay in one centre or were you transferred to others?

H: The place remained the same but charges against me changed. I was arrested on the charge of being a counter-revolutionary. The detention centre was No. 100 Dongshan (Dong mountain).

F: Where was it? Can you give me a brief introduction? I would like to enter it with you for a while.

H: I explained earlier that Huainan has nine districts and eighteen posts. No. 100 Dongshan is between the Jiulonggang and Xiejiaji posts, with the Bagong mountain to the rear. It's a very desolate area. There are no trees on the mountain, only earth and rock, and the wind regularly blows fiercely enough to blow away any saplings. The execution ground was in the hills not far away and the detention centre was situated in a kind of courtyard. The main entrance leads to the interrogation room through a small door. The building once belonged to the Public Security Department but during the Cultural Revolution, the public security organs, procuratorial organs and people's courts were rescinded, and the building came under the control of the military. The yard was full of prisoners but I never knew where the guards lived. The house number was 100, so it was called No. 100, Dongshan. The detention centre was at municipal level. The prisoners were quite mixed: there were thieves and criminals of all kinds, and there were prisoners kept there just before their executions. Some of the most important political prisoners of the Cultural Revolution were also there: An Ziwen, Minister of the CPC Central Committee Organisation Department; Li Baohua, son of Li Dazhao, who served as Secretary of the Anhui Provincial Party Committee, and some other high-profile officials.

F: Weren't there any other buildings nearby?

H: There was a camp for people to reform through labour. I don't know what happened there. It had nothing to do with us. And there were some peasants' earthen houses in the west which had nothing to do with us either. Sometimes we were taken outside the detention centre to cut hay and plant crops in the fields, and we could not see anything else. We were under extreme surveillance so that we couldn't escape. Oh, and there was a pond behind the house.

No. 100 Dongshan (after refurbishment)

F: Did you know that detention centres are not prisons? A detention centre keeps people after their arrest before they have been proved guilty. A prison incarcerates someone who has been pronounced guilty and they serve their sentence there.

H: I didn't know that. I never thought that I'd be a prisoner, would be arrested, or would be locked up. I felt that it was not much different from a prison though.

F: What were you thinking about when you were arrested?

FROM PURGATORY TO PARADISE

H: Death. I was thinking I might be shot or commit suicide. Didn't I have dozens of sleeping pills? I'll talk about that later.

F: What happened on the day of your arrest?

H: Just a casual conversation. The director–a woman whose name I did not know–talked to me in the interrogation room.

F: Why was a woman in charge of the prison?

H: I only heard that while working at Yan'an, she served as a maid to a top official, but I don't know how she got that job. At that time, public security organisations were a mess and there were two factions. Both wanted her to be on their side. She wore badges of the two different groups, one on each arm, as she didn't want to offend either. Wearing two different armbands made her look quite weird.

F: Was she cruel to you?

H: No, she exceeded my expectations. For almost a year, I'd met a lot of people who were as fierce as wolves and tigers, but she said to me: "Now you've come to my centre, don't think about anything — talk less, ask fewer questions and accept the sentence of reform through honest labour."

F: What did she look like?

H: She was slightly taller than average, slightly obese, quite ordinary really, but good-looking. She didn't like talking a lot, had a rustic appearance, treated people like ordinary country women do and was not aggressive. When we ate

HISTORY OF PURGATORY

our meals, she would join us and taste our food with a spoon, but this happened only when she was on duty. During her tenure, she also allowed prisoners' family members to send money and daily necessities. However, sending food was not allowed. You could read books and magazines, but they had to be revolutionary books. After she left the job, all these 'luxuries' were disallowed.

F: Did she ever abuse or punish you?

H: No. When I joined the detention centre, I didn't look like a human being because I had been beaten and bullied so much. She didn't ask me to do any hard or strenuous work. Anyway, she knew that I wouldn't be able to do it. She ordered me to write posters and slogans because nobody else there could. I was a very talented student of the Art Academy and excellent at writing Chinese characters. She treated me differently from the others because in Huainan there were hardly any people who had connections with the writers of *Sketches of a Three-family Village* and the Four Reactionary Writers. She looked at me differently and seemed to have some respect. There was no hostility or contempt.

F: It seems like they were treating you as an important person banished to a remote place.

H: Yes, it seemed a bit like that.

F: At that point, did you feel that No. 100 Dongshan was like hell?

H: Not then. On the contrary, I thought it was a safe place, a refuge. There was no thrashing or beating, no struggle

FROM PURGATORY TO PARADISE

sessions and we were given enough food. But that was only for a short period of time, when she was chief of the detention centre. After that No. 100 Dongshan was not like that for there was another person, whom I will never forget.

F: Who was that?

H: As I said, No. 100 Dongshan was a courtyard, and it was shaped like a square. Around this square-shaped courtyard there were numbered rooms for the detainees. On the outer side of the rooms, there was a circular veranda. On the veranda, there was a patch of cement where not an inch of grass could grow. It used to be extremely cold during the winter and scorching hot during the summer. From north to south, there were seven large rooms on each side, from east to west, there were three small rooms also on each side. My room was number 10 and it was a big room. It was around 3.7 metres wide and faced a big pit. Twelve people were crammed into this room. In the corner there was an open toilet. All the people in the room would shit and urinate in it. Although there was a cover, the fetid stink assaulted our nostrils. The window was very small, and it was covered with four layers. The first layer was glass, the second was wooden slats, the third was steel mesh, and the fourth layer was a grill. The grill worked like a blind: we couldn't see out, but the guard outside could monitor us. The four layers of the window meant that there was no ventilation, so the room was full of nasty smells. During the day, we sat close to each other by the pit with our backs against the wall. At night, we slept together—almost piled together. Newcomers were asked to sit next to the toilet, and then when others arrived, they shifted further away. The pris-

54

oners under sentence of death with handcuffs and shackles had to always sit or lie down in the middle of a row of prisoners, because people were scared about what they might do.

F: When you came, did you have to be by the toilet?

H: Yes, very close it. When I arrived, all the accused in the room stared at me. One old man, who was sitting in the middle said: "How come you have been beaten so badly? Can you take off your clothes so that I can see your bruises properly please?" After a few days, I learnt that this man was Ying Daitian, an army doctor with a rank of Lieutenant Colonel who had served with the Kuomintang (KMT). He was an octogenarian in good health with a great personality. At first glance you could see he was a cultured man. He was also a first-class doctor. At that time, however, he was tainted because he was a member of the KMT and so had been branded as a 'disguised spy'. He saw the wounds on my body and feet and immediately said: "Your skin is completely dark, the bones of your feet are broken and all out of place. If it's not dealt with soon, the bones will become useless."

F: Weren't there any doctors in the detention centre?

H: In that wild place? Where could there be a qualified doctor? There were only some emergency medicines.

F: Did he heal you?

H: Yes. He told the prisoners in the room that they should stop using their chopsticks for dinner and should give them

FROM PURGATORY TO PARADISE

all to him as well as any cardboard they might have. He used a simple and effective small splint method: he first arranged my broken bones, then supported them with chopsticks and used cardboard as a kind of splint. He was a military doctor, and military doctors are the best for traumatic injuries. Without his treatment, my legs and feet would've become useless.

F: What about your hand? Hadn't the tendons in your hand been cut so that you couldn't paint?

H: It's difficult to heal tendons. They got better in the course of time; I'll talk about it later.

F: You must feel thankful towards this gentleman; did you meet him again?

H: A year later, he was taken somewhere else; where, I don't know. But he left a deep impression on me—extremely self-respectful, steady, and fond of practicing *Taijiquan*[1]. He had his own style of doing everything.

F: You joined the army at a very young age and the education you received there must have been incompatible with KMT ideas. Were you on guard against him or even anti him?

H: Not at all. I was now a counter-revolutionary, and my crime was even bigger than his. I was confounded and could not understand who the enemy was and who was a patriot. Everyone was the same here. We were prisoners, but first, we were human beings.

HISTORY OF PURGATORY

F: At that time, did you have any doubts about society and your original beliefs?

H: To be honest yes, there were some doubts, but I was still rather confused. Doubt was certainly there, but having doubt was painful.

F: Denial is even more tragic. To deny your beliefs is like denying yourself and nobody wants to deny themselves.

H: Much more tragic was the situation of that Director Shi. She committed suicide.

F: Why?

H: It was said that the Public Prosecution Bureau denounced her and alleged that she was sympathetic to the prisoners and behaved like someone who was opposed to class struggle. She couldn't take it and cut her throat with a razor blade and died. There was another rumour that her boss in Yan'an had been overthrown. So, there was nothing left in life for her. She also could've been arrested and persecuted and so she ended her life herself. There were no more details. We didn't get real news in the prison. Everything we heard was possibly half-baked truth.

F: When was that? After a year?

H: No. It was in September 1969. Anyway, she'd already left for her heavenly home a few days before we came to hear about it. We'd been wondering why we hadn't seen her for some time and then learnt that she was dead. Frankly, I still miss her. She was very kind and innocent.

FROM PURGATORY TO PARADISE

2: EIGHTEEN LAYERS OF HELL

F: It is said that after Director Shi died you entered the depths of hell? Were you moved to a special cell?

H: No, I was still at Dongshan, still in cell number 10. It's just that when the prison director changed, everything changed. His surname was Yang. He had originally been the boss but left when the Public Security Offices were disbanded. After the suicide of director Shi, he returned. He was extremely cruel and vicious; he exuded a sense of danger just by standing in front of you.

F: OK, let's first discuss this person. Was he cruel by nature, bad or ultra-leftist? By ultra-leftist, I mean in his ideology.

H: Everything: ultra-leftist, vicious, inhumane and uncultured.

F: Ah, that's important to note. He was uncultured and on top of it, brutal. What did he look like?

H: Tall, thin, small eyes with yellowish eyeballs.

F: A pair of yellowish eyes—I have already got an impression about this person.

H: For four years, I was in his clutches. As soon as he came, our food changed. You can't imagine what rubbish we were eating. The vegetables were rotten, unwashed, and contained mud and sand. They hardly gave us any rice to eat. In the vegetable soup you would find bits of iron, tampons, condoms, and even shit 'capsules'.

HISTORY OF PURGATORY

F: What do you mean by shit 'capsules'?

H: These were constipated stools and even after being boiled in the pot they did not dissolve. Sometimes, we picked them out with chopsticks and called them 'Yellow Sauce'. We were accustomed to this and often made fun of it. We also called maggots in the vegetables 'vital protein'. Of course, all this was intentional. Director Yang used to say that we were class enemies. You must hate the enemy and be cruel to them. We were dying of hunger every day. Only when we were taken to the fields to cut the hay, could we have a picnic and catch insects to fill our stomachs. Bean worms, grasshoppers, dragonflies, toads— there was nothing that we didn't eat. When I used to catch a sparrow, I would just skin it, wash it and pop it straight into my mouth. Do you know what it is like to feel that sort of hunger?

F: I've heard about it from Zhang Xianliang and have read about it in the works of Cong Weixi[2]; now let's hear it from you.

H: When we heard the word "rice" we drooled. When we heard the sound of a bowl, we had goosebumps. Hearing the sound of a running electric motor in the kitchen was a huge pleasure. Once an administrator asked me to engrave a seal for him. I saw a half bowl of leftovers in a corner. It was just a mess and covered with long white hairs. But it was a life-saving meal. When he'd gone out, I immediately grabbed it and put everything into my stomach. Some prisoners were so hungry that they picked up cigarette butts and ate them.

F: Xianliang wrote that: "When you are hungry, you don't care about dignity." However, Mencius has said: "Even a beggar would disdain to eat trampled food."

H: That means he hadn't yet reached the point of extreme hunger. At the start of my time at Dongshan, I used to be taken very often for struggle sessions. Once after returning from one of these, my custody officer went to eat and locked me to a bicycle frame. He didn't give me anything to eat. I was sitting there hungry and dizzy. People looked at me as if I was an animal. I saw a lady holding a child who was eating a steamed bun. He was only eating the stuffing and throwing the bun on the ground. The steamed bun was extremely dirty, full of soil and ants from the yard, but I went up to it and grabbed it and immediately stuffed it into my mouth. At such a time, you don't think about dignity. What kind of dignity are you talking about? In Dongshan we had an Uncle Wu. One day, the criminal police brought him up for trial. The head of the criminal police got drunk. When he entered the room, he vomited all over the place...

F: Please stop. I can't really fathom this.

H: Dongshan detention centre had two giant dogs. They ate better than us. When we were let out for a while to get some fresh air, we ate all the food from the dogs' bowls when the dogs were away, and the officers were not very vigilant.

F: I don't want to talk to you anymore about eating.

H: Yes, well, I also feel uncomfortable when I talk about it, but I need to tell you. Don't you want to know the truth, my real experiences? OK, let's talk about something else. Let's talk about the person I just mentioned, Uncle Wu. I'll tell you more about him.

F: I'm listening...

H: Uncle Wu was a poor peasant. His full name was Wu Huayan but I'm not sure about the spelling. Prisoners weren't allowed to talk to each other and were threatened with having their fingers broken if they did. When Wu first came, he squatted by the kiln and didn't talk. He wore a cotton-padded jacket. He had only one tooth left, because of a serious fall. With just one tooth, it was even more difficult for him to eat anything. We asked a petty thief in the centre to take out his tooth with a thread so that he could eat with his gums.

Inside the courtyard of No. 100 Dongshan (after refurbishment)

F: How did he come after having a fall?

FROM PURGATORY TO PARADISE

H: Wu had come to the mines from a remote village to see his son. Both his son and daughter-in-law were activists and they had gone to the party school to learn; only Wu and the small child were at home. It was Lantern Festival day and he'd made some traditional sweet dumplings. He wanted to offer these first to Chairman Mao. Standing in front of a portrait of Mao he said: "Chairman Mao, if you weren't here, we the poor, wouldn't have these happy days. I'm not good with words. Please accept this bowl of sweet dumplings." As he spoke, he lifted the bowl up and leaned forward. Unfortunately, he slipped on some onion under his foot. He fell down and the contents of the bowl flew in all directions. When he stood and looked up, he saw a piece of sweet dumpling was glued to the eyes of the Chairman's picture. He went mad and asked his grandson to bring a stool, climb up and remove it. But the quality of the paper was extremely poor, and the sweet dumpling was wet, so when his grandson tried to remove it Chairman Mao's eyes got stuck down. Oh God! Unfortunately, at that moment some party workers came to tell him about a meeting. They saw Wu messing about with Chairman Mao's portrait and making holes in his eyes. They immediately arrested him and branded him a counter-revolutionary. The same day he was put on trial, sentenced to three years, and was sent to reform through labour. When he was leaving, he secretly told me the story with tears in his eyes: "Three generations of my family have all been poor peasants; how could we oppose Chairman Mao?" What could I say? He gave me a jar of food to eat. There was some rotten pumpkin in it. He could neither eat it nor take it away, so he gave it to me.

HISTORY OF PURGATORY

F: Were there a lot of absurd incidents like this?

H: Yes, quite a few. One man bought a bust of Chairman Mao and was carrying it on his bike. It wasn't easy to carry, and he was afraid it might fall off, so he tied it with rope to the handlebars of the bike and was caught "tying up Chairman Mao". Oh, and there was another worker in our factory who tried to make a bust of Chairman Mao as was the fashion during the Cultural Revolution. But our factory only made big clay bowls and we never made any porcelain busts. As the men had no experience and poor material, the busts were often crooked or distorted and they wouldn't stand upright. When this worker was putting his bust of Chairman Mao into the kiln, he realised it was not straight and said: "You are crooked! Let me correct you, you are crooked!" Unfortunately, the Party Secretary was standing behind him and heard him. He immediately arrested him, calling him a counter-revolutionary and claiming that he had scolded, offended, and insulted Chairman Mao.

In the detention centre at Dongshan there were all kinds of people—thieves, murderers, rapists, and violent criminals. Since the Cultural Revolution, the number of counter-revolutionaries had gone up exponentially.

F: Had they all been sentenced?

H: If they had been sentenced, they were sent to the reform through labour centres first.

F: How long was your sentence?

H: I was never sentenced so I was kept at the detention centre. I spent a total of four years and seven months there.

63

FROM PURGATORY TO PARADISE

F: If you hadn't been sentenced, how could you be kept there for such a long time?

H: What wasn't possible then? Detention could be indefinite. Is there a deadline in the cowshed? Was there a deadline for the May Seventh Cadre School?[3] Nobody took our lives seriously.

F: Did anybody die in custody?

H: Oh yes. There were two groups of people. One was those who died inside the centre because of physical or mental illness. There was a man who suffered from uraemia and couldn't urinate. He was ignored and choked to death. The other group lost their lives through the death penalty. I'll tell you about the death penalty later.

F: Ah! Why have you stopped?

H: ......

F: OK, let us change the subject. Let's talk more about your life in the detention centre. Your room was so small. How did you keep warm in the winter?

H: There wasn't any heating and it used to be freezing cold in the winter. But winter was better than summer. If it was too cold, we could squeeze together tightly. Summer was incredibly difficult to bear. The room was airtight and with the toilet bucket inside, the air was very fetid and sour; I can't describe the smell.

F: Could you do anything about this?

HISTORY OF PURGATORY

H: No, there was no escape; we had to put-up with it day after day.

F: There must have been loads of mosquitoes then!

H: No, you are wrong. There weren't any mosquitoes. And not only no mosquitoes, but no bedbugs and no lice. Why? Our blood wasn't good enough for even those insects to suck it. It was a kind of miracle. We were all extremely skinny with no muscles. When I was released from the centre, I weighed only 36 kilos. I could measure my waist by spanning it with both my hands.

F: Couldn't you buy anything?

H: Who'd buy things for me? And where would I have got the money? At the struggle session at Huainan Literary and Cultural Centre, that beautiful lady had put ten yuan in my pocket. I asked the guard to buy me some toothpaste and used it very sparingly each day for fear of running out.

F: And didn't you bring anything of your own when you came?

H: One day, after I had asked for them, I was thrown a pillow and some ragged clothes from my old factory. Those were all my belongings.

F: You are a proletarian in the true sense. How did you spend the Chinese New Year Spring festival and your birthday?

H: Did we need to celebrate New Year or our birthdays? We didn't even know what date or month it was. Occasionally from the loudspeaker broadcasting in the distant villages we

FROM PURGATORY TO PARADISE

could hear that it was New Year, or National Day, but it had nothing to do with us.

F: Were you granted any special allowances?

H: Yes, a bath. We could only bathe once a year. They would put 61 centimetres of hot water in a cement pool of 12 square metres. When the inmates went in, the hard skin on their bodies flaked off like fish scales. After one batch of people left, another batch came in and soon the water would turn into a dirty white milky soup. Normally there was no hot water but when it was steaming hot, some people couldn't bear the shock. Once a man died and was carried away from the pool. I didn't bathe in that sort of water anyway. I used to wipe my body every morning when I washed my face. It's impossible to imagine how dirty that bathing water was. There were all sorts of people among the convicts, and nobody knew what kind of diseases they were carrying.

F: Were the convicts based there permanently?

HISTORY OF PURGATORY

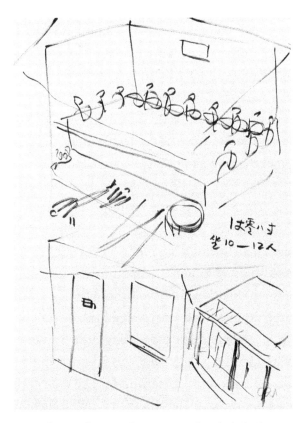

Schematic diagram of No. 100 Dongshan (painting by Han Meilin)

H: No, it was a detention centre. Those who were condemned to death were taken out to be shot without our knowledge, while petty thieves were imprisoned for some days and then released. There were some in temporary custody who were taken away within a few days. Nobody knew who the other inmates were; nobody cared about anyone else. Occasionally I would hear about some bizarre happenings and weird people which you'd never hear about in the outside world. One day, for example, two men were brought in. Both were soldiers. One was old and the other

FROM PURGATORY TO PARADISE

was young. The younger one was short and fat, and was crying all the time. We didn't ask but they told us everything. The young soldier was, in fact, quite famous. He once removed a sleeper that some evildoers had placed on a railway track, saving all of the passengers on the train, for which he was praised by the central leaders. Later, though, it was somehow revealed that the whole incident was a fake and that it was he himself who had placed that sleeper on the railway track. At the time, no one else knew about it. After he was received by the central leaders, he wanted to be a 'hero' again. So he put a big rock on the train track himself and waited so as to move it as soon as the train came. But this time the train driver saw everything from a distance and immediately applied the emergency brakes. He got off the train with a spade and started hitting him. The soldier was then arrested by the police. This was a very serious act as it was deceiving the central government. The case of the older soldier was even worse. He was the regimental commander and a colonel. He had played chess against a private and lost several games in a row. The private was extremely proud of this and was dancing for joy. This enraged the regimental chief so much that he took out a gun and shot and killed him. The colonel was sentenced to death. The young soldier's red badge of military merit was taken away and the regimental commander's uniform was stripped off. Both these men were taken away after only two days in the detention centre. Would you hear of or meet these kinds of people outside? Those who were sent to the detention centre were extreme and wicked people. But I'd done nothing, and I didn't have the interesting history these guys had. I hadn't committed murder or arson. I hadn't molested a woman or

HISTORY OF PURGATORY

done any sort of damage. I'd never done anything bad to any person, society or the country. Why were they keeping me there? Who could I confide in? I felt completely hopeless, but I didn't commit the ultimate sin of despair.

F: You were not reconciled?

H: Though I sometimes I felt hopeless, I was not reconciled.

F: Good. Perhaps that way you learned to value life.

3: FEMALE PRISONERS

F: Were there any female prisoners at no. 100 Dongshan?

H: Yes. Women came mostly because of their illicit relationships with men. At that time, any sort of illicit relationship was illegal and even criminal.

F: How many women? How many cells?

H: Just one small cell with six or seven inmates. Sometimes fewer, sometimes more.

F: Were the supervisors of the women's cells male or female?

H: Male. In the past, there had been the female superintendent, Shi, but after her there was not a single female officer. The women's cell was the heart of the detention centre so, whether it was a male detainee or male warder, their eyes were all fixed on it.

F: In a place where humanity is lost, only the nature of a beast remains intact—food and sex.

H: The male prisoners used to look forward to the time when the female prisoners were let out to relieve themselves. Listening to the chirping voices of the women was very satisfying for them. In that kind of place, every female prisoner is beautiful to male prisoners and male warders. Their laughter was like silver bells; when they came out with the pots or talked among themselves it pierced our hearts. The women prisoners were aware of the vile thoughts of the male prisoners though. After all, they were not very virtuous women themselves. Now they intentionally became even more provocative. They went barefoot, wore short skirts, and flashed their supple thighs. They seemed to show off their sexuality; every single male prisoner was excited.

A high wall at No. 100 Dongshan (after it was rebuilt)

F: Male and female prisoners were not allowed to go out and have some fresh air at the same time. Is that so?

HISTORY OF PURGATORY

H: The men were able to do all sorts of things: they squinted through the crack behind the blinds of the window in the cell. A thief also used a needle to make a bean-sized hole in the window flap to peek at the females.

F: What about the wardens?

H: It was much more convenient for the warders: everything could be seen from the outside, especially on the hot summer days when the women took a shower.

F: Was it true that you could all have a shower once a year?

H: When the weather used to be extremely hot, females could wash themselves inside the room. All the guards would peep through the window as though they were watching an erotic movie. The women knew they were being watched, but they didn't give a damn. Let them watch —after all, one day all of them would get punished. One day the girls urinated in a plastic tub in the cell and started shouting: "Help, somebody is seriously ill." As soon as the guard opened the door, they threw the tub of urine over him. The guard was drenched in yellow water and foam but remained silent out of shame.

F: Perhaps, only the female prisoners could teach a lesson to the guards?

H: Please do not think in this way, as the power was still in the hands of the guards. Sometimes they would take the female prisoners for trial. The interrogation room was quite small. While the one guard was strolling outside, the other would rape the woman.

71

F: That's so cruel. Why didn't the female prisoner sue them?

H: The guards would give them steamed bread to eat. That way she wouldn't say anything to anybody. Sometimes the guard would rape her while she was actually eating the bread. They were all extremely hungry; after getting the bread, they wouldn't say anything.

F: The most deformed trade between food and sex!

H: Among the women prisoners, two stood out. Both were very beautiful. One, whose surname was Wang, was quite plump and well-proportioned. She'd been a nurse at a hospital at a mining machine plant. Her father was a party cadre officer at a very high level. But her life was a complete mess and she was in an illicit relationship with a doctor. She was later shot because she had had an affair with a rebel faction leader, who was said to have died while having sex with her. People said that the girl had killed him.

F: He might have died due to a heart attack.

H: I'm not sure. Some people said she didn't kill the rebel faction leader, and that she was being rehabilitated. But what was the point of rehabilitation when she was shot for being a murderer? When the van was taking her body for burial to Bagong mountain, I saw her face and she was certainly very beautiful. It was said that after the shooting, some idiots even pulled down her clothes and separated her legs with a wooden stick. Because she was so beautiful all the morons wanted to see her private parts.

HISTORY OF PURGATORY

F: This is completely unthinkable today. A girl's life was handled at will. She must have shouted for justice at that time, but who would have paid attention in those days.

H: The other woman prisoner was called 'Big Sexy'. She was very tall and white with long legs and looked very sexy in a Western way. That's the reason everybody called her Big Sexy. She had been a cashier in a grain store and seemed an extremely nice woman. However, she was also very randy and had all kinds of casual relationships, and she was also involved in corruption while dealing with the grain coupons. At the time she was arrested, she was found in a compromising position with a manager on a pile of grain. Not only was she immoral, but she was also quite mouthy too. Once, she was walking in front of a cell and a man shouted: "Big Sexy, I love you!" She laughed and immediately retorted: "I, your great-aunt, have got nothing for you. The long dick your great-aunt might have seen will be enough for you to suck."

F: This shows she was a loose woman, but also that she was capable of displaying a sort of intemperate conduct when in a hopeless situation.

H: Think about it. What was the difference between the sexes? Men and women all became Adam and Eve, naked in body and soul. Can you imagine what a totally different world I was living in?

F: I'll talk about that at the end. Did you know what finally happened to Big Sexy?

73

FROM PURGATORY TO PARADISE

H: She spent 20 years in prison.

F: It should be said that here you not only tasted but also witnessed the darkest and ugliest aspects of society.

H: I also saw the most shameless and obscene things. There was a lot of scum among the prisoners. I can't tell you everything, but I'd like to talk about a person who gave the saddest impression.

F: Was it a female?

H: No, he was a young lad in his twenties and a former soldier. At the start, he was a guard for General Xu Shiyou but later he was told to work in the mines. He was under the death penalty because he'd killed a man during an altercation between two-factions. In this armed struggle, there wasn't always a conviction: not all Red Guards who had killed several people were convicted. However, the opposing faction seized power, arrested him and he was sentenced to death. He was locked in our cell and wouldn't eat or drink. He cried bitterly and said he'd obeyed orders from the Central Party Committee. Hadn't the party asked for 'Offence by Pen and Defence by the Sword'?[4] But it wasn't any use saying this and he was definitely going to be shot. He wrote six letters in his defence to General Xu Shiyou but they were all torn up by Prison Director Yang with the yellowish eyeballs.

F: Was he really gunned down?

H: A few days later he was shot. On the day of his execution, Director Yang came with some other people to the cell. Zhou shouted: "I am only 23. I read about 'Offence by Pen and Defence by Sword', the clarion call of Jiang Qing, in the newspaper *Wen Wei Po* and acting on the advice of the Central Party Committee, I took part in the armed fighting. You can't kill me. If you spare me, I can do lots of good things." Director Yang slapped his face and shouted: "Motherfucker, you're going to die soon and yet you're talking like this!" His face was covered with blood and it's difficult to talk about what happened next.

F: If this incident left a deep impression on you then you must tell me.

H: It's OK, I will go on. Zhou went to the toilet in the corner of the room, lifted the lid and shouted: "I'll tell you this. I'm not married, and I've never touched a woman. I'm going to be a shameless creature now." I can't continue further.

F: It was extremely terrible, wasn' t it?

H: Guess what he did? He undid his zip, took out his thing and started masturbating. Then he put down the toilet lid, tightened his belt and said: "OK, let's continue; I'm married now." He suddenly became quiet, not noisy any more, and his face was surprisingly calm. Do you know why?

F: He suddenly understood everything. Like he'd had a big awakening?

H: Looking at his expression, I thought so.

F: If that was the case, he could at least die in peace.

H: At that moment, everybody in the cell went quiet. Zhou walked out with his shackles banging on the ground, and as

FROM PURGATORY TO PARADISE

soon as he got out of the cell, a policeman punched him twice in the ribs, completely winding him, and then he dragged him into the car and took him away. He was only 23 years old, a few years younger than me.

4: FAKE SHOOTING

F: Was there any particular turning point in your life of suffering? Did you ever think of suicide?

H: Yes, I did. Twice.

F: Can you tell me about both the times?

H: The first time was when the sleeping pills were discovered and the second was during a fake shooting.

F: By 'fake shooting' do you mean a situation where you were taken with the culprit to the place of execution and, while the culprit was executed, you were left alive in order to be intimidated? In my book, *Ten Years of Madness: Oral Histories of China's Cultural Revolution*, I wrote about an eight-year-old who was intimidated along with the convict.

H: Yes, you're right. You are made to accompany the condemned to the place of execution.

F: Let's talk first about the sleeping pill incident. Were these the sleeping pills you brought back when you went to Hangzhou to ask Cai Xiaoli for a certificate in the initial years of the Cultural Revolution?

H: Yes. As I told you earlier, I'd witnessed the fate of Gai Jiaotian. I'd felt the murderous spirit of the Cultural Revolu-

HISTORY OF PURGATORY

tion. It didn't bode well for me, since I was a counter-revolutionary in the eyes of revolutionaries. I was scared; I was quite feeble then. My later tenacity came after constant struggle. You remember that on the way to Hangzhou I went to Shanghai to see my mother. My sister-in-law worked at a hospital and I told her about my insomnia. She gave me some sleeping pills, but I asked for them repeatedly and, in this way, I piled up a whole bottle of almost seventy-two tablets. After returning to Huainan from Shanghai, I hid the tablets inside a pillow.

F: So, how come these tablets reached the detention centre?

H: After I was arrested, the warden asked the factory for my bedding and they brought it. As I said earlier, one day the guard threw my pillow and clothes into the cell. As soon as I felt the pillow, I knew the sleeping pills were still inside. I touched the pills and felt a special sense of security. I thought if I couldn't bear it any longer, there was a way out.

F: But suddenly a cell-mate found this out?

H: Yes, you guessed right. A thief in the cell found out that there was something in my pillow. After he realised what it was, so as to earn 'brownie points', he reported it to the superintendent. As soon as Superintendent Yang heard about it, he called me and said: "Thinking about suicide is counter-revolutionary. If I don't punish you, you won't realise the severity of it." The method of punishment that he chose for me was extremely painful.

F: How painful?

FROM PURGATORY TO PARADISE

H: First, he asked someone to take me to another cell and asked the convicts there to deal with me. There were several kinds of convicts in that cell—hooligans, thieves, those who had injured people in fights. They were extremely ferocious and were experts in beating people up. They kicked the base of my spine so hard that it swelled like bread. Then one guy took me out of the cell and made me kneel on the concrete floor in the courtyard without my legs touching my buttocks. I wasn't eating healthy food at that time and had no strength at all. I was extremely skinny, just a bag of skin and bones. I was forced to kneel down, not for two or three hours but for the whole day and night. When Yang saw that I was completely incapable of doing it, he dumped me back again in the cell. My back was hurting so much that I couldn't sit down; I could only lie on my stomach on the brick-bed. Do you know what I wanted to do at this juncture?

F: Not live any longer?

H: Exactly the opposite! I didn't want to die; even if you'd given me the sleeping pills, I wouldn't have swallowed them. From Huainan Porcelain Factory, where I was arrested and the bones of my hand and feet were broken, to the day when I knelt on a hard cement floor, I had a firm belief and conviction in my heart that I wasn't going to end my life myself. I had produced something against society. The more they harassed me, the firmer my conviction was to live. I was determined not to die. Isn't life a one-time gift? On what basis could other people decide if I lived or died? I was determined to live. I not only wanted to live and feel the power of life but also keep my self-esteem.

HISTORY OF PURGATORY

F: I believe that this was a turning point, rather a sublime turning point in your life. It was an extremely important episode for your future. When did you get the same kind of feeling again?

H: When I was taken to a fake shooting.

F: Ah! You had such a terrible experience. As I said just now, I wrote a chapter in my book *Ten Years of Madness: Oral Histories of China's Cultural Revolution* entitled *An Eight-year-old Death Penalty Accompanier*. That was an oral history which I wrote in the 1980s. It was about the Cultural Revolution in Kunming, Yunnan province. The protagonist of that tragedy was an eight-year-old girl who had no idea what the death penalty was about. Your tragedy is that you knew exactly what the death penalty was, and what execution by shooting was. Please tell me about it. Why did they want you to accompany the condemned man?

H: I don't know.

F: How did it all start?

H: Superintendent Yang wanted to scare me. As I told you earlier, the prisoners in our cell were allotted their seats based on their arrival date, but condemned men would always be given middle seats so that there were people on both sides to silence them.

F: Was there any special mark on those who were awarded the death penalty?

H: The condemned had to wear heavy handcuffs and shackles. A pair of cast iron shackles and chains could weigh 19

FROM PURGATORY TO PARADISE

kilos. Zhou Jicheng had been wearing shackles and hand-cuffs all the time.

F: Was there a fixed time for shooting?

H: No. Nobody knew what day the crime inspectors would come. They didn't shout out names, they pointed and said "You, You, You". If you were pointed out it meant death was imminent. They dragged you out and shot you.

F: But you were not awarded the death penalty and you did not wear any shackles or handcuffs.

H: One night, the criminal inspectors suddenly barged into our cell and pointed at me, saying: "Come out!" I knew it was going to be terribly bad. I was pushed into the yard and told to bend down and was immediately covered with a jute sack. From a tiny hole in the sack, I could see there were two other people who were also covered with sacks and were kneeling down. We were then pushed into a vehicle. It was pitch-black and we didn't know where we were going. It was all too sudden, and I didn't understand what was happening.

F: You did not think at all about the 'shooting', did you?

H: No. I was not sentenced to capital punishment and had not committed any heinous crime to merit a death sentence. The car stopped at the foot of a hill. The criminal inspectors pulled us out and told us to stand side by side. They kicked us and we knelt down. They were all very experienced.

F: Did they kick the calf muscle?

HISTORY OF PURGATORY

H: Yes, they kicked me at the back of the knee (showing the exact place) and however strong you are, you have to kneel down, if kicked there. Then they lifted the sack off and I could see clearly. I was sitting between the two culprits. In front of us there were gunmen and I thought I was going to be gunned down.

F: How were you feeling at this time?

H: You might think that I was so terrified that I was going to piss in my pants. But it wasn't like that. Until you face that sort of situation, you don't know how you're going to react. I thought I was going to leave the bitter sea of human life. I didn't think of anything else except that I was going to be free.

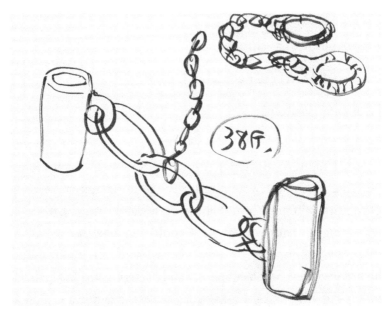

Shackles and handcuffs worn by death-row prisoners (painted by Han Meilin)

F: Did you think there wasn't any future for you? Did you think about your mother?

H: No. It was as if there was a vacuum in my brain and I was already dead.

F: How did the shooting start?

H: I just heard somebody saying: "Don't wait any more. Fire!" I heard a very loud and shrill sound and the man next to me fell flat on the floor. His blood and brains drenched me, and in that moment, it all felt like too much to bear.

F: What happened to the person beside you?

H: There was the shrill sound of another bullet. That was to kill the other man, but I didn't realise it at the time and I thought it was to kill me.

F: Did they fire the third bullet?

H: They did but I did not realise it at all.

F: Did you pass out?

H: Yes. Then they fired the third bullet and I couldn't fathom it out. I fainted and when I opened my eyes, I saw blood both sides of me. It was pitch-black and I thought I was in purgatory. But how could there be a moon in purgatory? I was lying on the ground. All I could see was the sky. And there was a moon in the sky. I heard someone talking but how could that be possible? I bit my tongue and felt pain. I didn't know whether I was dead or alive. My mind was in a total whirl.

HISTORY OF PURGATORY

Later, I was again thrown into the vehicle and dumped at the detention centre. When I was pushed into the cell, all the inmates were frightened to death. A man covered in blood. I was drenched in the blood of those two who'd just been shot. I'd blood on my hair, face and mouth. I said to the others: "Don't be scared. I'm Han Meilin".

F: How did they react?

H: When they understood the situation, they took off my clothes and wrapped me in tattered towels and a quilt. The next day they washed my clothes during the leisure time and hung them outside. Several days later, when the clothes were dry, they allowed me to dress. When I put on my clothes, I felt extremely uncomfortable as the blood had not been completely washed off and there were still clots of it on them.

F: Who decides who'll be the companion at the execution? The law certainly doesn't allow this sort of penalty.

H: Was there any rule of law during the Cultural Revolution?

F: I don't know. In that case, it must have been decided by Superintendent Yang. Did he enjoy so much power?

H: Of course. That's the kind of place it was. "When the cat's away, the mice will play." There was no hope left. He enjoyed great power, deciding life and death. A demobilised military officer, who had been wrongly arrested, couldn't take it any longer and wanted to escape over the wire. Yang called people to strafe him with a machine gun. Accompanying the condemned prisoners for the 'final show' was just a method to frighten us.

83

FROM PURGATORY TO PARADISE

F: You said these two incidents had huge transformative effects on your life; why was that?

H: As I see it, that wasn't a fake shooting, but a real one.

F: Yes, you died once. How do you see death? Or let me put it this way: what will death mean to you in the future?

H: I no longer fear death. I've died once.

F: These two experiences have had a significant effect on you. Once for life, once for death. The first experience made you believe strongly in the power of life, the second one made you not afraid of death. Was it like a great awakening for you?

H: No, I'm a great fool with a blind allegiance to foolishness. Do you understand what I mean?

5: THE LAST THREE SENTENCES

F: Now let's change the subject and talk about your spiritual life. I think it's impossible for a person like you who was born to paint, to be alive and have no spiritual life.

H: Aren't you going a bit over the top? I said just now that while I was lying on the ground at that execution place, I saw the moon. Do you think I dreamt of meeting the beautiful Goddess of the Moon?

F: I'm talking about your inner or spiritual life. While you were in isolation, did you think of any woman, perhaps one whom you loved a lot?

84

HISTORY OF PURGATORY

H: Do you mean my wife? She reported me to the officials and eloped with another man, one who also wanted to expose me and who was in her power. While I was in Dongshan, my wife wanted a divorce. When I saw the solicitor's letter, I said nothing and signed it immediately.

F: Did any other beautiful women leave a deep impression on you?

H: At Huainan art troupe, a girl had put Rmb10 and a food coupon for ten kilos in my pocket; she'd left a deep impression on me. At a time when everybody was deserting me, why did she behave in this loving manner? She didn't even know me.

F: Perhaps it was because of your talent. Didn't they see your paintings?

H: More because of her kind nature. Perhaps it was basic instinct.

F: The most important attribute of a woman is a kind nature. Was she pretty?

H: Absolutely gorgeous. Her name was Cheng Meimei. I learnt about her when I came out of prison.

F: Who else did you think about?

H: My 'Son', the dog who stuck with me in the most difficult and turbulent phase of my life. His backbone must have been broken after that thrashing, and I didn't know whether he was dead or alive. When he pounced on me with his two front paws and scratched me lovingly, it left a mark on my

FROM PURGATORY TO PARADISE

clothes. I was unwilling to wear those clothes in case I erased the marks. But later when all my other clothes became rotten, I had no option but to wear them.

F: You had no clue about him, had you?

H: I was isolated from the world after being locked up in Dongshan but when I was released, he was the first thing I tried to find.

F: Could you read the newspapers?

H: The detention centre rules didn't allow access to information from the outside world. Occasionally we heard news from the distant loudspeaker broadcasting. Once I heard that *Anti-Dühring*, written by Friedrich Engels, was an encyclopaedic work of Marxist political economy. I thought that as they considered me an anti-Marxist-Leninist, I should read it and learn more and see if I was anti-Marxist-Leninist or not. I had some money and I appealed to the authorities to get this book for me.

F: Buying books on Marxism and Leninism should've been fine, shouldn't it?

H: Director Yang tore up my request and said: "You can only read the book *Quotations from Chairman Mao Zedong*.[5]" Later an official bought me the book. I remember it only cost 75 fen and I learnt a lot from it.

F: I've read the Engels' philosophical work *Dialectics of Nature* and appreciate his ideas. How much Marxism and Leninism did you learn from *Anti-Dühring*?

HISTORY OF PURGATORY

H: I realised that the Cultural Revolution was not in tune with Marxist-Leninist ideology, let alone the Communist ideal.

F: The Cultural Revolution was opposed to all civilisations in human history and was anti-civilisation and anti-human. The Cultural Revolution era was certainly a reactionary one. If you'd been asked whether you wanted to read books or paint, would you have still chosen to paint?

H: It's not a matter of what I would have chosen to do because, believe it or not, I was already painting.

F: But you didn't have anything. How could you paint? What about paper? You didn't have any brushes either.

H: Chopsticks were my brushes, and my trousers were my paper. I used to put *porridge gruel* on my trousers, and when it dried, I used chopsticks to make white marks. Every day I'd do this. If there wasn't any *porridge*, I'd apply some soap. Do you know why I like to paint with *sable* brushes these days? It has something to do with my painting with chopsticks. The *sable* brush is harder. However, if you paint regularly on your pants, they get ripped. If my trousers were ripped, then I had to patch them. Therefore, there were always patches on my trousers.

F: What did you paint?

H: All kinds of people with different kinds of faces would regularly come to our cell; they all became subjects for my sketches. I also loved to paint from my imagination.

87

FROM PURGATORY TO PARADISE

F: I said earlier: "A person paints to reflect his soul." Whatever you painted, they must all have been outstanding pieces of work. Even at those times you still preserved the freedom of your soul. Autocracy can only curb people's actions, not their souls.

H: But autocrats always try to control people's souls. Wasn't the Cultural Revolution a "great revolution touching people's souls"?

F: What did painting mean to you?

H: I'd another purpose for painting too. They'd damaged the tendons in my arm so that I would never be able to paint again. I just wanted to exercise my arms and did so continuously for four years and my arms got better. You see, although my hand is a little crippled and a muscle is missing, I can still paint with ease.

F: You're a symbol of victory against those who are anti-art, anti-human. It could be said that today every piece of your work is a sweet fruit of victory. Did anybody in your cell know that you were painting?

H: They didn't know and weren't interested either. Even if they saw me, they thought I was just killing time with random doodles.

F: You didn't have a bosom friend or confidant here, did you?

H: They didn't understand drawings and paintings, but they liked me telling stories.

F: What kind of stories did you tell them?

HISTORY OF PURGATORY

H: I'd read a lot of books: novels, novellas, dramas, legends, and stories from movies from ancient times till the present, both from foreign countries and from our country. But to be honest, I made many of them up. They loved all my stories, but they liked romances best. These filled a hole in their hearts. Some days, even after nine pm when the lights were switched off, I would still be telling them stories. The guards would also stand beside the window and listen with rapt attention. I could see their shadows from the window.

F: Stories are born when people are poor in spirit. I also used to tell stories during the Cultural Revolution. When you tell a story, you're exercising your imagination. In a cell, the land of spirituality becomes desolate, so your stories were indispensable food for your fellows.

H: My stories made me a kind of spiritual leader' in the cell. They really listened to my advice on several matters.

F: This was a kind of abnormal and poor spiritual life.

H: But in a long and endless life of uncertainty, just relying on storytelling and painting on trousers was hard. You can't live like that and I sometimes felt hopeless and couldn't see any light at the end of the tunnel. After three years, every day seemed very long—a day felt like a year.

F: It seems that the only option was to become emotionless.

H: That was very hard to do as reality would regularly intrude. For example, after the Lin Biao incident of 1971, people's craze, foolishness and determination toward political movements cooled down. Several of my friends in Huainan, who were painters or other artists, somehow

FROM PURGATORY TO PARADISE

heard that I hadn't had a square meal for more than three years. They managed to take me out for a meal after contacting a manager named Tao at Dongshan.

F: How was that possible?

H: Tao was a very kind man and perhaps because he had a good relationship with one of my friends, he managed to do it.

F: On what pretext?

H: Illness was used as a pretext. I was only a bag of bones so they said I must be taken to see a doctor. You could be let out to see a doctor and, as Tao wielded some authority and power, my friends took me to a restaurant in a department store where nobody would recognise me. They ordered all kinds of delicious dishes: chicken, duck, fish, beef, everything. As soon as I saw them, I started crying.

F: You became emotional.

H: No, I was a bit naïve. When I saw them, I thought that the central authorities in Beijing must have known about my condition and learnt about the injustice inflicted on me. I started crying. Wasn't I stupid?

F: How could you think in this way at this time?

H: Well, I was a really naïve person at the time. A bit daft, you might say. My friend Jiang Menglin said to me: "You've become almost like a ghost; why are you thinking in this way? The central authorities are not bothered about you. We've arranged all this." These words made me realise the reality of the situation and I started crying again. But this time it was different: I was crying because I knew the truth. I cried so much that I couldn't eat what had been so ceremoniously laid out on the table.

F: You have an unempathetic side to your personality which people can't understand very well. Your artistic IQ is excellent, but your IQ regarding relationships is not that great. As Mo Yan[6] has said, you are rather an 'inattentive' person. Maybe this is a facet of your lovable nature. Maybe you're completely engrossed in your painting and forget about other things. Foolishness is also a kind of simplicity. I've always believed that only a person like you, with such a simple disposition, can take art to such incredible heights.

It seems that the date for your release from the detention centre was getting closer. You were released in 1972, weren't you?

H: I was afraid that if I was confined any longer, I'd never be able to get out. My body had completely collapsed. The manager had already seen that I couldn't stand it any longer. He stopped asking me to go out to work. He would ask me to sit in the yard for a little longer each day and bask in the sun.

F: You're echoing what Engels wrote in *Dialectics of Nature*. He said that when human life was on the verge of collapse, there would be no warmth left in the sun. People would rush to the equator and would try to get some warmth, but it would be weak even there.

H: We were given a haircut every four to five months. Hair grows very long in four months and they would cut a lot of

FROM PURGATORY TO PARADISE

hair off. Afterwards I would feel as though the hair I had shed hadn't fallen off my head but had floated down. The hairs were very thin and long, and yellowish in colour. Hair is a symbol of good health. I felt that I wasn't going to survive for long.

F: How did the director treat you?

H: On one occasion, the director asked me and a guy nicknamed Idiot Hu to move a huge urn from one side of the yard to the other. The mouth of the urn was one metre in diameter and the weight was more than fifty kilos. As a skinny person with no strength left in my body, how could I lift it? I passed out when I exerted myself. I had to rest under the shade of a tree for a long time and then I was able to regain my strength and stand up. I was suffering from malaria at the time. I couldn't eat anything at all and was on the verge of death. Director Yang told me to sleep on my own in a small empty cell as he was afraid that I'd infect the others. However, he didn't trust me. He asked two petty thieves to sleep in the same cell and keep an eye on me. Three people sleeping in one cell was not very crowded. On National Day each prisoner was given a small piece of meat, but I couldn't eat so I gave my share to the two thieves. I didn't even want to eat meat. I'd no strength left and thought I was near death.

F: How was your malaria treated?

H: There was a deputy director, Ren, who gave me a quinine tablet. I was surprised that it cured my malaria instantly. Maybe it's like the saying "when a person is in the last phase of life, he can live on a drop of water."

HISTORY OF PURGATORY

F: Perhaps it was because you hadn't taken medicine for a long time. Medicines are very effective for people who rarely take them. I want to know if you had felt something before you were released?

H: I didn't dare to think that way as I thought I had no future. But one day when I went to cut the hay, Director Yang told me: "After you're released, you can go to many places and do well; you just need to change a bit." I was totally surprised to hear this. How could he be talking like this in such a mellow tone? Was I going to be released? Even this thought was like a flash of light in my mind. People who've been in distress don't think very optimistically, they always think about pain. But not long after, to my utter amazement, I was released.

F: When was that?

H: 7 November.

F: Who told you?

H: Director Yang. He called for me.

F: Did he call you for a conversation?

H: He called to trap me.

F: I don't quite understand.

H: The director told me: "We're letting you go. Tomorrow, your office will take you back. You've spent a lot of time here. Whatever grievances you may have, mention them here. Don't talk about them outside. If you mention them here, nothing will happen to you."

FROM PURGATORY TO PARADISE

F: Definitely a trap. If you'd said you had any grievances, they would've been considered as criticism of the dictatorship of the proletariat, and you wouldn't have been freed. Releasing you was not in his power; it was an order from the top. He had to obey the order. But if you said anything about what had happened to you, he would have reason to lock you up again. That man was vicious.

H: Do you think I'd been suffering in vain for so many years? I was not so naïve now. Didn't I know he was trying to trick me? I wasn't going to be fooled by that guy.

F: So, how did you react?

H: I said that I'd say only three things. One, I'm not an anti-revolutionary. Two, I'm not an enemy of the people, and three, even if you give me a gun, I'm not going to shoot anybody.

F: What did he say?

H: He couldn't reply to that. I thought I'd been really smart to cross over this *'ghost gate'*—the gates of the prison.

F: It seems you could protect yourself. You weren't in prison for nothing. Of course, the fee you had to pay for this long detention was unreckonable. You could say that this sort of 'smartness' is taught by fate, just as many animals have an instinct for self-protection which is automatically triggered in a dangerous environment. Is this the tragedy of our generation? Will the present or the next generation understand us? Will they think we are a bunch of miserable creatures? But if the current generation had been raised in those times, what would they have done? It's

HISTORY OF PURGATORY

one thing to evaluate that era; another thing to have experienced it.

The day after your release—8 November 1972—must have been a very significant day for you. What did you feel after you had been set free?

H: I can't really express my emotions after my release. I left toothpaste, toilet paper and ragged jackets for my inmate-brothers, and the '*Red Book*' as well. The prison officials were standing beside me so I couldn't say anything to my companions. A petty thief winked. To the felons who would be executed by shooting, I gave them a touch on the shoulder. When someone gets released, everybody thinks about their own fate, their own future.

F: Did anybody from your ceramics factory come to meet you on the day of your release?

H: A junior colleague called Yin went back with me. I completed the formalities and got back all the stuff that I'd handed in when I was taken to the detention centre. The belt was rotten and useless. The photo on my identity card was faded. The small carved wooden figure which looked like a Korean girl was still there and I picked it up. There was also some money. When I left the detention centre, I can't say what my feelings were, but I noticed that compared to when I arrived, all the tiny willow saplings outside the centre had become big trees, and a young yellow calf had grown into a big cow. As soon as I stepped onto the bus, I realised that I'd returned to the human world—a Paradise. I was thrilled to hear a child crying, a bicycle bell ringing, and a hawker shouting, selling something. I felt human again. I saw wonton sellers, cigarette sellers, people walking in the streets, and heard traders shouting loudly. I hadn't heard these things for more than four years. I was glad to be back on the human planet. But I had no energy. I walked for a bit and then sat down to rest for a while. I still had some money on me, so I decided to buy a packet of biscuits to eat. I didn't expect the biscuits to be so hard. I hadn't eaten anything hard for nearly two thousand days. In the cell I had *porridge soup* every day. I couldn't chew any more; I couldn't eat the hard biscuits. My mouth hurt and I vomited blood. Later a doctor told me that it was just as well that I couldn't eat biscuits, for some prisoners came out and ate a lot of food and died within a few days. Their stomachs had shrunk, and it was hard for them to digest food and so they died.

F: This is indeed unheard of!

H: When Yin had taken me to the security department, he'd told me about the "three restorations": that my job was restored, my wages were restored... and there was another one, but I can't remember it now. The factory was also quite good to me: they gave me a six square metre room to live in.

F: You told me earlier that the first thing you wanted to do after you were released was to look for your 'Son', the dog.

H: Yes, I had some money with me, and I immediately bought some meat and went to look for him.

F: I have written a story *Thank You, Life* where I mentioned you trying to find the dog with a piece of meat. I also wrote that you finally met the dog.

H: Actually, I couldn't meet him. When I went to Yang's house, he was frightened to see my thin, small, inhuman and ghostly look. I said: "Don't be frightened, I'm all right and back at the factory. I haven't come here to see you; I'm looking for that dog." Yang said that the dog's backbone had been broken on the day of the incident at the shame parade and he died after two days of whining. He threw the body away without burying it properly.

F: Ah! So, you didn't even know where to go and say a prayer for him.

H: But I'll never forget him. He died for me; he died so that I could live.

F: Does your love of painting dogs relate to Son?

H: Dogs are more faithful than humans. I say "faithful" because they'll never betray you. Have you ever heard of a dog betraying its owner? Therefore, I always draw dogs. My painting *Friends in Adversity* is about Son, so that he'll always remain in my heart.

F: I remember it was considered a masterpiece a few years ago. It's a moving piece of work. If people knew your story, they would love it even more.

After your return to the factory, did your colleagues still consider you a villain?

H: It was much better. However, the Cultural Revolution hadn't ended and from time to time after getting support from senior political leaders, it gained momentum like a wave. Also, I wasn't completely rehabilitated yet and was

FROM PURGATORY TO PARADISE

still working in the Huainan Porcelain Factory and hadn't yet returned to Hefei, so I got mixed up in politics at times. There were still a few people in the factory who wanted me to be put to death. They supported political movements and hated seeing me still alive. For example, when the "Criticise Lin Bias, criticise Confucius"[7] movement started, they supported it and smashed my products whenever they had the opportunity. When the movement came to an end, they came back to me and asked me to do designs or write banners for the workshops. But my junior colleagues were very nice to me.

F: How did you feel?

H: It was very easy to recognise their affection for me. They expressed it very simply and directly and used to send me things to eat. I was alone without any family so when they brought me food, I felt very happy and sensed their warmth.

F: Did you have any girlfriends?

H: I didn't have a relationship with any women in Anhui for 22 years. There was one girl named Song Zairong who appreciated my work and she used to come sometimes to my small studio to chat with me. We became closer. At that time, young men and women were very simple in their relationships. I used to give her a lift on my bike to a nearby street. She sat on the rear seat and put her arms round my waist. Somebody saw us and told her father. Her father had known me before and didn't have anything against me, but because I wasn't yet rehabilitated and free from all charges, he was afraid that his daughter would have no future with a counter-revolutionary. So, he firmly opposed our friendship

HISTORY OF PURGATORY

and even beat me up. Her brothers also came and attacked me. They brought some other men to beat me up and this caused me a lot of trouble for a while. My factory colleagues stood around my house to protect me. Later Song Zairong was transferred to work in the municipal government, and it wasn't appropriate for her to be friendly with me, so the relationship came to an end. Because I was a 'political problem' I didn't have any more girlfriends; I didn't want to bring trouble to others.

F: Did you ever meet up with Cheng Meimei of the Huainan Cultural Group?

H: Yes, I went to see her, but she was already married. After I was released, the actors and artists in the Huainan Arts and Works Group and some other people who liked paintings often came to see me. I used to carve some small animals like kittens, dogs, chickens and foxes, apply colour to them, and give them as gifts to them. I also used to draw for them. Everybody was appreciative and very happy.

F: What kind of paintings did you do?

H: At that time, if you were a figurative painter, you were only allowed to paint workers, peasants and soldiers, but I didn't. It's easy to make a mistake and be accused of distorting the image of workers, peasants and soldiers. I just used to draw all kinds of beautiful flowers and lovely animals and everyone liked them. Paintings of animals and birds were scarcely produced at that time.

F: That's right, it was thought of as "bourgeois leisure" painting. Did you do any traditional Chinese paintings?

99

FROM PURGATORY TO PARADISE

H: I didn't have any rice paper, so how could I do traditional paintings? I created a new kind of painting, 'water brush painting'. I'll tell you more about it later. I also invented a pen stroke that pulls out the 'tongue' behind the tip of the pen.

F: 'Tongue'? To guide the ink?

H: Yes. In this way, you could draw multiple lines at the same time and the effect was very special. I also began to practice calligraphy and research classical Chinese characters.

F: How did you do this? You didn't have the necessary books.

H: It was a matter of a blessing in disguise. All my good fortune has been brought to me by adversity. At the end of 1972 I was asked to write a big-character poster for the factory, and I fell off a desk. Didn't I break my leg at the beginning of the Cultural Revolution? Now my leg was fractured again. The department of osteopathy at Huainan Hospital was not very good, so the factory workers sent me to my hometown, Jinan, and my classmate, Zhao Lin, took me to the biggest hospital there. Fortunately, this hospital had excellent orthopaedic doctors. They realised immediately that the broken bones were out of alignment. If the doctor hadn't forced the bones apart and fixed them properly, I would've been lame for the rest of my life. When the bones were knitted properly, I went to Shanghai to my mother's place to recuperate. I'd been particularly weak since my release, so I used to walk and bask in the sun every day. There was a second-hand bookstore on the Fuzhou Road where I often used to go and indulge myself with the books. One day, I found a pile of old unclassified books in a corner. It seemed that the words on the cover of one of them were staring at me –*Classification of six categories of Chinese characters*. I asked the shopkeeper to hand it to me. When I touched it, I felt cold and was trembling all over. Then I started crying and could not stop.

F: Why?

H: Because this was a valuable book for researching classical Chinese characters.

F: How did you know the value of this book?

H: It must have been fated because when I was a child, I often used to go to the village temple to play and sometimes I used to take out a book which was kept behind the main statue in the temple. I wondered who had hidden it there in the first place. It was a book explaining the characters inscribed on bronze vessels during the Shang dynasty.[8] Although I couldn't understand much, the characters and pictures amazed and fascinated me. I used to write the characters in my notebook, or rather what can be called my esoteric writing. This was more than thirty years ago and now I saw this book. I'd suffered so many hardships between then and now, and had almost lost my way with art. Why wouldn't I become emotional and cry? I held it tight, close to my heart.

F: You are indeed an angelic person.

H: The shopkeeper sold me the book as he could clearly see how much I wanted it. I had some money from when I was rehabilitated. Later, the bookstore continued to sell me other ancient books such as *Zhou Dynasty Inscriptions, Bronze Inscriptions,* and *A Thousand Characters in Four Shapes.* Reading these books and learning from them became my main hobby in Huainan. Calligraphy has nothing to do with politics, so calligraphy and the study of ancient literature became an integral part of my life.

"Missing Home". Han Meilin's hand painting of his early years in primary school classmate Zhao Bin's home. The painting was completed by Han while he was recuperating from his injuries.

F: It seems your life became a bit better now.

H: In the latter period of the Cultural Revolution, there was intense fighting among the top politicians and there were fewer mass movements, so I was much more relaxed. The factory gave me a very tiny studio of a few square metres. I designed some tea sets and sculptures. The factory didn't

HISTORY OF PURGATORY

produce this sort of thing, but it didn't prevent me doing them. I made them and gave them away. The atmosphere was certainly much more relaxed.

F: Was there any other kind of albatross?

H: Of course, there were some encumbrances. I hadn't been cleared of all the charges yet and hadn't returned to Hefei. I was initially banished to this factory as a punishment.

F: That kind of pressure is invisible. I've also felt it. Before the end of the Cultural Revolution, no one could see the light at the end of the tunnel. Although the peak was already over, nobody knew when the end was coming or when it might pick up again. We had to be very careful and maintain a very low profile.

H: I used to get up at five o'clock every morning and go on my bike to Bagong mountain to practice *taijiquan* with some friends to recover my strength. At the weekend people used to rest and there was no one in the factory. Then I went to Bagong mountain on my own but instead of doing *taijiquan*, I used to climb to the top and cry bitterly looking at Shouzhou.

F: Why did you used to cry?

H: Because I had no relatives, no close friends and felt completely devastated. My heart ached and my future was uncertain, so I needed to express my inner feelings. On the top of the hill, I was alone and could cry. Every weekend I used to go to the top of the hill and cry there desperately.

F: How long did this continue?

FROM PURGATORY TO PARADISE

H: I did this until the Cultural Revolution ended.

F: I can imagine your situation. I can sense that after the frightful billows and terrible waves of your experience, as well as a close escape from death, you were finally blown to the shore by the winds and waves of the times. You were bedraggled but you survived. You have the attributes of a legendary character.

3
RETURNING TO THE
HUMAN WORLD AGAIN

1: THE HUMAN WORLD

F: You must remember when you came back to Hefei even though your life has been full of nodes of life and death.

H: Of course, I remember. It was in 1978 and I was forty-two years old.

F: You began your burst of art, didn't you?

H: Yes, and as soon as the Gang of Four were eliminated, my problems also ended.

F: Was that when you were in Huainan?

H: Yes. As I said earlier, the new painting style that I created called 'water brushing' had been widely appreciated. Demand for my paintings soared and people from all walks of life asked me for more pictures.

F: It was not a market-oriented time. People didn't buy paintings, but they wanted them. Your water-brushing

FROM PURGATORY TO PARADISE

painting was a revolution. It was different from Chinese painting on rice paper where such a vivid 'fluffy' style can't be created. It was also different from watercolour drawing. You can't properly use a Chinese brush and ink in watercolour. You really created a completely new kind of painting. I was stunned to see your work for the first time: 'fluffy', elegant, energetic - and the use of magical Chinese ink—simply incredible.

H: It was the product of suffering. I wanted to paint but I couldn't find rice paper. However, there were many types of drawing paper in the Arts and Works Group. I remembered that in watercolour painting you can use a technique of brushing liquid on the paper before painting. I mainly used ink instead of colour. The effect was unique. Gradually I developed this way of painting. If there'd been rice paper at that time, I wouldn't have brushed water on the paper, and I wouldn't have created this style. So, as I said, huge suffering forced me to create this sort of painting.

F: Is the technique very complicated?

H: Like traditional Chinese painting, the most important thing is to fully understand and balance the mixture of ink and colour. Ink on paper brushed with water dries very fast. As for technique, you get to understand it after constant trial and error. Let me give you some details. At the beginning, I wanted a way to make the ink 'splotch' but couldn't do it. For example, pandas' eyes are white. When you paint the eyes, you mustn't allow the ink to seep into the white. How could I resolve this? Once while painting a camel, a boy stood beside me and looked at it interestedly. He liked the fluffy camel I was painting. Pointing at my picture, he called several people to see it. He touched the picture with a finger and perhaps there was some oil on his finger because the colour stopped flowing outwards. This gave me a brilliant idea. I'd found a way of preventing the ink from seeping.

First photo after release from jail

F: Did political pressure on you decrease?

H: At this time a new factory director, Qin Zhongming, joined us. He recognised my talent. He was open-minded and ordered me to stop working in the workshop and specialise only in design and organise my time myself. So, I could paint freely, and my work caught the attention of a wider audience. A man called Chen from Guangdong Institute of Light Industry invited me to paint traditional plants and flowers for them.

F: Did the factory agree to this?

H: It was the beginning of 1977. The whole country was sharply criticising the Cultural Revolution and many people had already started rehabilitation. I went to Guangzhou and did several hundred traditional paintings of plants and flowers for them. They also printed a collection of my paintings and called it *The Flowers of Mountains*. This was my first collection of paintings to be published. Not long after this, Wan Li returned to work as the Party Chief of Anhui province and he immediately gave an order for the rehabilitation of Yan Fengying, who was known as the queen of the 'Huangmei opera'[1]. Yan Fengying was wrongly accused and committed suicide like many intellectuals did during the Cultural Revolution. The literary and art circles were unfrozen. Writers like Chen Dengke, Lu Yanzhou and painter Xiao Ma were also rehabilitated. They were all great masters of Anhui province.

F: I know Chen Dengke and Lu Yanzhou very well. They're both excellent writers. Lu Yanzhou's *The Legend of Tianyun Mountain*[2] had a huge impact at that time.

H: Later Chen Dengke and Xiao Ma came to Huainan for an interview. They heard about me, looked at my paintings and then immediately called me to a meeting with them. They went back to report to the Provincial Party Committee about my paintings. Somebody told me that Chen Dengke also wrote to this committee to ask for my rehabilitation. In the autumn of the following year, Huainan city held a citywide cadre meeting, at which it announced that they would comprehensively rehabilitate me, transfer me to Hefei and allow me to join the Federation of Writers.

RETURNING TO THE HUMAN WORLD AGAIN

F: So, you were exiled from Beijing to Hefei, then you were sent from Hefei to Huainan for reform through labour and then you were imprisoned in Dongshan. Fifteen years later you returned to Hefei after a close shave. Have you ever wondered why you paid so much for nothing and experienced such a terrible life-and-death crisis? You don't have to answer now. I'll talk to you about it later when we get to the next part of your journey through life. From documents about you, I know that in the year when you were rehabilitated, you started working very hard. You painted everywhere, gave art lectures and published your works.

Cooperating with Lushan Yi of Jieshou Ceramics Factory

H: Yes, I couldn't stop myself.

F: 1978 and 1979 can be called the periods of "volcanic eruption" in Chinese literary and artistic circles. I call it

FROM PURGATORY TO PARADISE

"breaking the ice", like the thawing of the completely frozen Yellow river. When glaciers crack, they often make loud noises and huge chunks of ice wash ashore and flatten villages. I wrote a memoir of the Chinese literary world from 1977 to 1979 and called it *Jumbled Ice*. It was an unforgettable era. An outbreak of spirituality under high pressure is uncontrollable and creative power is immeasurable, so a great new period of literary and artistic movements began. I myself wrote around 700,000 Chinese characters in 1978 and felt my emotions surging out. We immediately became famous all over the country. It was at this time that your water brush paintings stunned everybody, especially in 1979 when your exhibition was held in Beijing.

H: Huang Yongyu was the first to hold a large-scale one-man exhibition after the Cultural Revolution. I was the second. Several stalwarts from the cultural field including Feng Mu, Huang Yongyu, Bai Hua, Ye Nan and Hua Junwu came to support me. My painting *Once Again a Brave Man After Twenty Years* was presented to Bai Hua, as we'd both shared the same fate. *Lonely and Cold Alluvium* was presented to the singer Zhang Quan. She was exiled to the bleak northeast of China during the Cultural Revolution.

F: You were finally discovered, recognised, appreciated and loved by the whole world. Your life changed dramatically and in 1985, when government policy changed, you returned to Beijing.

H: Because many friends helped me. Most notable among them were Chen Dengke, Xiao Ma, Zhang Guangnian, Feng Mu, Tang Dacheng, Wu Taichang and Chang Shana who

RETURNING TO THE HUMAN WORLD AGAIN

said: "When our Central Academy of Arts and Crafts sent Han Meilin to Anhui, it was to help set up an Academy of Fine Arts there in three years. How many years has it been now? He must be completely rehabilitated". She spoke resolutely and emphasised "complete rehabilitation". I'll never forget them.

F: They were all excellent people. I admired Chang Shuhong[3] and Chang Shana[4]. We are alive today because of those great souls.

H: Xiao Ma helped me a lot in Hefei. We lived together in a small building allocated by the Provincial Party Committee. Xiao Ma was a real artist. He had a good command of painting, music and literature. Living with him was like living with live art. His daughter, the writer Yan Geling, was also a good friend of mine.

F: The writer, Yan Geling?

H: Yes, she was very spiritual. She had not written anything at that time, but she had a good understanding of art.

F: It was another world when you returned to Beijing, wasn't it?

H: When I returned to Beijing, I began to launch a comprehensive fully-fledged blow on art ...

F: I was a witness to that. We've known each other since the 1980s, and we've been in constant contact ever since. I've seen many of your important artistic activities and large exhibitions, the completion of your three art galleries in Beijing, Hangzhou and Yinchuan, and I delivered a speech

FROM PURGATORY TO PARADISE

before the inauguration of each one of them. I've always attended your annual birthday celebrations and academic forums. I've also admired your love for your wife, Jianping, and your unique and colourful family lifestyle. What's important is that I've seen how easily you crossed over from one field of art to another, and constantly created new genres. Am I right?

H: Yes, you are.

F: I'm becoming increasingly interested in researching you. The most important thing is the history of your soul and the deep composition and core of your art. But I wanted first to discover your biography. Next, I want to explore the impact of your experiences on your mind and personality. I believe that a real artist's work is the externalisation of his soul and character. Our current research on artists only focuses on their works, not on them as people so my research on you must start from a human perspective.

2: LIGHT AND SHADOW

F: You're one of the most unfortunate artists I've ever known and one of the luckiest too. You've been in the harshest, coldest, most ferociu and inhuman layer of society. No. 100 Dongshan was the most bizarre and outlandish place. But you were lucky and didn't die during the dark times. You stood up after the cruel dark night and started running to the art world as you so desperately wanted. Brightness and darkness equally occupy half of your life. What is the relationship between them? That's what I want to discuss with you. Although you can't see the darkness of yesterday

RETURNING TO THE HUMAN WORLD AGAIN

in today's light, has it gone? Has it become a hidden shadow, or has it been transformed into part of your character and art, or even helped in the success you've attained in both? I've been searching for the answer relying on my personal observation but today I want to know directly from you.

H: If you are interested, I am willing to narrate. What do you want me to talk about first?

F: Firstly, do you still have any grievances about the injustice you suffered?

H: I forgot everything in the latter days of my Dongshan time.

F: That's because of several cases, as well as those incidents of kneeling and fake shooting. That last time in Dongshan, when your friends picked you up for a meal; faced with a table of chicken, duck and fish, you thought that even the Central Party knew you'd been wronged. As a result, you woke up from a dream and blind loyalty disappeared. Right? The loss for the initiators of the Cultural Revolution was that they have lost large numbers of "blind loyalists". What a practical revolution needs are not "blind loyalists", but firm believers. When those blind loyalists woke up, what happened? In fact, there had been progress because blind loyalty belongs to feudalism. But I wonder whether, after the collapse of the blind loyalists, had you lost hope for society?

FROM PURGATORY TO PARADISE

H: No. After their collapse, I was exonerated. I should mention that after the end of the Cultural Revolution, instead, I had real hope for society.

F: The Cultural Revolution taught us what kind of society we needed—a healthy, fair and civilised one. That is something our generation felt strongly. For example, Zhang Xianliang, who had been in prison for more than two decades, was rehabilitated. One night at Nie Hualing's home in Iowa, USA, we were having tea and talking about Deng Xiaoping and China's reform and future. At that time, we were all very excited and full of hope, and our eyes were sparkling. The year was 1985, the year when with the change in government policy, you returned to Beijing. Well, let's not talk further about this but return to the original topic and to Dongshan as I want to dig deeper. In the most desperate times, when you hadn't an iota of hope left, did you believe in Fate?

H: Yes. Initially I thought a lot about it and often contradicted myself. I knew that I came from a very poor family, had joined the army at thirteen, was devoted to revolution, had some ambitions and was going in the right direction. Although I complained sometimes, what had happened wasn't my fault. Didn't the rightists say you should argue with them but not bludgeon them? But the Central Academy of Fine Arts and the Fine Arts and Crafts Institute bludgeoned many rightists. Also, I hadn't done anything counter-revolutionary. When did I become a traitor and pass important materials to foreigners? From Beijing to Anhui, from Anhui to Huainan labour reform, and then in Dongshan prison, I suffered so much, but why? What for? I

114

RETURNING TO THE HUMAN WORLD AGAIN

couldn't find the answer then and I could only put it down to Fate—as if such a disaster was destined to happen to me and I couldn't escape it. Putting it down to Fate made it more bearable and so it didn't cause a lot of mental trouble. It was the only option I had.

F: Then, you could only curse your fate!

H: Do you have any other option?

F: So why did you use chopsticks to draw on your pants? Why did you try to heal the broken tendons in your hands so that you could paint again?

H: Well, I'm not sure but perhaps it was basic instinct. Didn't I tell you earlier that I was perhaps born to paint?

F: So, you're saying that there's nothing in your life except painting?

H: I guess so.

F: What I cherish most in your history of suffering is the image of you crouching in a cell, hungry and cold, and still drawing on your pants with chopsticks. Perhaps even you didn't know why you were doing it. Maybe you were just obeying your basic instincts and nature. Painting was more important for you than even your life.

H: Maybe you're right.

F: I'd like to discuss with you now the relationship between suffering and character. When I was writing *A Decade of One Hundred People*, I found that there were two opposite kinds of educated young people. One kind was crushed by the heavy pressure of life and disappeared from history; the other kind was shaped by blows from the hammer of life. You see, among the social elite—the backbone of society today - there is a group of powerful figures who were young during the Cultural Revolution. A hard life crushes the weak but strengthens the strong.

H: I've said earlier: "Some people wanted to destroy me with suffering, but in the end, suffering shaped my life."

At Huainan Porcelain Factory in 1974

F: I think you've got strong moral integrity. You don't bend but on the contrary always dare to stand up and hold on to your beliefs. Do you agree?

H: Yes, morally I am very strong.

RETURNING TO THE HUMAN WORLD AGAIN

F: Were you born with this morality and fortitude?

H: As I was born in Shandong province, I was deeply influenced by Confucianism[5] from my childhood. People should be modest, honest, affectionate and righteous. As a child I was extremely shy and was embarrassed to eat at other people's homes, so I was always a bit hungry. Once I went to a house and they gave us nice vegetables and rice. I put the rice bowl under the table, and it was gulped down by a dog. On induction day at the Central Academy of Fine Arts, the dean made a speech and the students also expressed their views. Each one of them said that they wanted to become an "engineer of the human soul". I wasn't good at speaking and was the last one to speak. I showed my modesty and said that I had no soul. Everyone laughed. But after decades of suffering, I changed, and my personality also changed. In Dongshan, I was punished for hiding the sleeping pills by being made to kneel down for the whole day. I felt I was being tortured, but I couldn't even commit suicide. From then on, I wasn't afraid of anything. Not only did I want to live but I wanted to live a real life. I survived like that. Don't you think my personality has changed because of all this?

F: This reminds me of Aleksey Tolstoy[6]'s saying: "Heated in three waters, bathed in three bloods, boiled in three lyes, cleaner are we than clean." In your case, it should be changed to: "Boiled in three lyes, bathed in three bloods, and burnt in three fires, cleaner are you than clean ."

H: You can see why my painting of a horse is different from that of Xu Beihong. You can see my robust nature in my paintings.

F: Sometimes there is an explosion, a kind of inner irresistible force. Sometimes it's reflected in your paintings. In fact, all your personality is in your paintings and your destiny also appears there. But the sordid and sad things of Dongshan have never appeared in your paintings.

Displaying "Friends in Adversity" painting

H: It's impossible to conceive of a situation where there's no shadow of that in my heart. I still have a problem with my lower spine: it still bleeds and is an unfortunate legacy of my imprisonment. The older I get the more painful my beaten and broken feet become. Occasionally, I have nightmares about my days in Dongshan. But when I'm engrossed in the world of art, it's different. Artists should live in the realm of loveliness, be detached from their emotions, not produce ugly things, but beautiful things and give hope to people. As soon as we find a thing of beauty, we should express it in our art.

RETURNING TO THE HUMAN WORLD AGAIN

F: At the same time, your art isn't entirely sterile. Your animals and plants are very tender. I'm afraid it has something to do with thinking about your misery when you paint these images. You idealise and humanise them. Is your painting idealistic? In the history of literature and art, idealism is the product of a barren spirit of reality. Can I ask you one last intrusive question? Do you think about your past?

H: Yes, I do sometimes feel nostalgic. Sometimes I would invite those who had helped me during that painful time to Beijing. Friends from Hefei and Huainan, ordinary workers, including those who helped me in Dongshan. I invite them to come and enjoy themselves at my place. I organise a group tour to visit East Asian nations or Europe. I always miss them and thank them wholeheartedly.

F: Do you miss those miserable years? Life in No. 100 Dongshan?

H: Of course, I miss them but obviously I don't miss the suffering. I miss those years as they can never be reclaimed.

F: I understand, it is part of your life, and it's also part of your art.

PART TWO
PARADISE

Paradise is not very far from us.
It depends how tall we stand.

FENG JICAI
Author

CONVERSATIONS IN THE KINGDOM OF ART

I FIRST CAME TO KNOW HAN MEILIN shortly after he'd emerged from his time of misery but hadn't yet returned to Beijing. Perhaps it was 1983—I can't remember the exact date or occasion. Anyway, he was already famous by then. When I first saw his 'water brushing' painting, I felt that it was innovative and unique. The first impression I had of him was of an unattractive short man with a pale complexion, but his eyes were very bright and penetrating, and there was something pure about his personality, like he was opening his door to you without any scruples–there was a light inside which made people directly feel his innocent nature. I was deeply impressed by his vision; it remains the same even today.

I gradually became friends with him, knowing that he'd endured extreme hardships and humiliation. Today you can easily see a mark on his right wrist which he got when a man pierced his tendon with a knife during a struggle session. It left a scar and looks terrible. You can imagine the tragedy of it. During our conversation, he told me to touch the scar. When my finger touched the bump, I felt a sort of pain in my heart. I was curious: how could I not have seen anything in his face before, especially in his eyes which were not dark and doubtful but, on the contrary, very clear and frank. What makes it even more incredible is that the same is true of all his art—free from mist, light—pure beauty. I often ask myself, is it his nature or has he successfully achieved spiritual transcendence? Where's the bitterness that's always been painful to swallow been hidden? If he's deliberately hidden it, then why? With my writer's professional hat on, I've always used his spiritual history as the object of my study. I secretly pay attention to the things that he inadvertently reveals, trying to find out the reality behind them.

Even after all his suffering, his life hasn't been very peaceful and calm. He experienced failure in his married life and huge physical distress. At the same time his artistic achievements have brought more and more laurels, but they've been accompanied by various personal troubles. However, his natural pursuit of happiness, frankness, and willingness to make friends, fondness for fighting for righteousness and just causes, coupled with his constant high output and his continuous artistic innovation, have made his life colourful after middle age. But these aren't my main concerns.

My concern is the relationship between his fate and art; the relationship between darkness and light; and how he entered the paradise of art after heavy suffering.

In the previous part of the book, *Purgatory*, I told the history of his suffering pretty clearly. In the next part, I shall still use the oral method and ask him to tell us about his own *Paradise*, his 'World of Art'. It's difficult to sum up Han Meilin's art because he has dabbled so widely, diversely and independently, constantly updating his works and even subverting himself. I want to clarify this world of his art, including the composition, source, essence, concept, advocacies and style. I want to find out what kind of home he built in the paradise of art.

So, there are some differences between the two parts. The first part is his oral biography, mostly events and experiences, and so subjective. The next part is his spiritual world, mostly analytical and cognitive, and more objective. However, both parts are the cause and effect of Han Meilin's life— a magical cause and effect—just as day and night are linked, and darkness leads to light.

In the first part I tried to explore the reason he could later enter Paradise and in the next part I want to explore the deep meaning of fate to his art.

Of course, this kind of thing can only happen to a real and pure artist. I've written:

"Real artists are saints who use their lives to worship beauty."

———

F: Now let's start with a whole new topic we're both keenly interested in: your art and your 'Kingdom of Art'. For this reason, I've chosen to hold this conversation at your Museum of Art in Beijing. There's a superb collection of your beautiful works here. In such an atmosphere, I will think more actively, and inspiration will come naturally. I want to discuss your art in your Kingdom.

H: Not a bad idea. It may spur new thoughts. But calling this place a 'kingdom'—you flatter me.

Feng and Han in conversation

F: After returning to Beijing in 1985, you started to fulfil the ambitions that were burning inside you even before 1964; 1985 was a golden year for the new era of literature and art. All kinds of restrictions on new ideas were lifted and all kinds of literary and artistic talent joined hands. Many batches of excellent writers and artists emerged. Many experimental novels appeared as did the literature of reflection and another literary trend of critical realism. The

CONVERSATIONS IN THE KINGDOM OF ART

literary scene at that time was exceptional and full of vivacity. At the same time, the world of art also started to expand. Experimental contemporary paintings had an impact. The first contemporary art exhibition was held at the China Art Museum in 1989 and it stunned society. At the invitation of Gao Minglu[1], I went to Beijing from Tianjin to cut the ribbon for the inauguration of the exhibition. It was an exciting time. Foreign literary and artistic thought influenced Chinese literature and art, and gave it a brand-new significance. Different kinds of thoughts and opinions started to emerge and gained favour in society.

In such an environment, you, Han Meilin, seemed to be out of this world and immersed in yourself. You just did your paintings, sculptures and ceramics and created your own world.

I think that when you were creating your unique world, you were ahead of the times so nobody could understand you, to be honest, not even I me. I could only see that you'd your own unique way of doing things and you did those things independently without seeking support from anybody. You didn't join any fashionable clique in the world of painting, and you didn't engage in any obscure or fashionable trends. But gradually your art shone out everywhere and you got immense recognition. People knew about you and said: "Yes, this is Han Meilin's work." It wasn't just about style for all your work has striking symbols. At this time, you started broadening your horizons; you were busy with various projects, from paintings to esoteric writing, from sculpture to modelling—you shone in various fields and created a magnificent world of your own with an

FROM PURGATORY TO PARADISE

incredible number of fantastic works. In this world there are people like you with strong personalities and similar artistic characteristics, so that's why I use the word 'kingdom'.

I've given myself the job of analysing your kingdom theoretically, but this has added some pressure. Your kingdom is rich and huge and, although there's been some critical analysis of it, no one's done a comprehensive and holistic study of it, so naturally I feel the pressure.

I'm delighted to talk to you in the presence of your works for Han Meilin, who has lived in the eighteen layers of hell, now sits in his own paradise, and talks about art from his heart. I think my readers will also read about this with great interest.

Where should we start to understand this kingdom?

1
AN INQUEST INTO THE KINGDOM OF ART

F: I've described your whole world of art as the 'Kingdom of Art'. You mightn't accept this and think I'm exaggerating but I do so for two reasons: one is the magnificence of your works—so many genres so that it is extremely difficult to compare you with anyone else; the other is that you have a personal aesthetic domination over your art. I can call it a 'kingdom', but I can also call it your 'World of Art'.

H: Calling it my World of Art is too kind of you, I think.

F: What I want to know is: is your World of Art intentionally constructed? Or is it a result of natural accumulation over a period of time? Writers write individual works and gradually form their own 'literary world'. However, some writers set up a grand goal at the beginning, such as Balzac who wrote the novel *La Comédie Humaine* in 97 volumes, and then they create their own vast literary world.

H: I've gradually evolved because of my nature. No one can predict exactly what will happen tomorrow. There are all

FROM PURGATORY TO PARADISE

kinds of uncertainties ahead and it's impossible to set our dreams too high. I just wanted to be a good painter and an honest person. I didn't want to be a great painter or a very noble person. I could only make a small effort to prove my ideology to be true and I wasn't sure about my future.

F: Our understanding of art is like climbing a mountain. When we reach the peak, we can see another higher peak in the distance.

H: Every step forward in art must come naturally.

F: I see what you mean: don't try to make yourself taller by pulling your hair up.

H: In life as well, there wasn't any way to elevate myself.

F: Do you think it'd be OK to remove any genre, such as calligraphy or sculpture, from your World of Art? Would that make your World imperfect?

H: Of course, it would. All of them are equally important for me. I can't remove any.

F: I reckon your World of Art has four major characteristics: the first one is painting which includes various genres; the second is esoteric writing, including calligraphy; the third is sculpture and the fourth is design. Your dyeing and weaving, ceramics, woodcarving, glassware, sand-fired pots, and so forth, I've put under the category of design, both 'shape design' and 'pattern design'. Do you agree?

H: Yes, I do.

F: Are these four categories equally important to you? Is there any one more important than the others, such as painting?

The maestro at work

H: No, all of them are equally important. The 'most important' doesn't exist. Whatever I wanted to do, I did; whatever problems I encountered, I tried to solve. I often made fun of myself. Sometimes it was unpredictable—I didn't know what I wanted to do. I would get up, go to the studio and when I was near my drawing board, I wouldn't know which part of my brain would be activated and make me change my mind. Maybe I'd paint, maybe I'd start writing, maybe I'd completely change my mind, get into my 'caravan' and go to the countryside. When I became unpredictable because of my mental health issues, I didn't view my work

FROM PURGATORY TO PARADISE

in terms of what was 'most important'. What was important then? Whatever my brain told me to do from one of the four categories you just mentioned.

F: Your creations are certainly unique. In Chinese painting, 'Nine Immortals'[1] are required. In the Six Fundamental Principles of Painting[2], isn't there a sentence referring to the *business position*'? Do you do a rough draft?

H: Not regularly. I've accumulated a great deal of experience and when I see blank white paper, my head is generally empty, and I'm not sure what to do. But as soon as I get out my brushes, everything comes naturally into my head.

F: Are you very impulsive when you go into your studio?

H: Yes. The feeling is very good.

F: Is there one aspect of art which you value more than the rest?

H: No, because they all come as a whole to me; they're like 'four brothers'.

F: 'Four brothers' is a good description. Brothers are born from the same mother; none of them can be separated from the others.

H: They influence, constrain and complement each other. Perhaps I can explain. For example, when I paint, wild grass comes to mind; when I design a sand-fired pot, painting is also a part of it. A new experience in one area naturally leads to progress in another area. You also said it right—which of them can be divorced from the other?

132

AN INQUEST INTO THE KINGDOM OF ART

F: When you're engaged in linking creative works from one area to another, is there any rationale? From what I've just heard it seems that there isn't. Perhaps it depends on your mood.

H: Yes, my mood. But as I'm a person whose thought jumps around, sometimes I can't control myself. For example, when drawing the head of a bull, different and strange thoughts about bulls' heads would constantly come unbidden into my mind. From painting a bull's head, I would jump to painting a human body and a variety of beautiful human bodies would emerge. I knew that the things coming out at that time were all fantastic, and I would keep on painting, do as I please.

F: I remember that once we went to a meeting at the Great Hall of the People. Suddenly you picked up all the paper from the nearby seats and started drawing different tigers. Why did you do that?

H: To be honest, I'm always short of time to do things. I was fifty when I returned to Beijing. My youth had been spent in reform through labour camps and prison. I could only use chopsticks to practice drawing on my tattered trousers in the cell. So, when I had time on my hands, I had to paint all the time. A friend of mine knew that I start drawing as soon as I see paper. I was visiting his house once and he put a lot of paper on the table beside me. I sat down and automatically pulled out a piece of paper and started drawing on it. When I left his house, the pile of paper was finished, covered with drawings.

F: Are you going to grab back the lost time?

FROM PURGATORY TO PARADISE

H: Because I was not allowed to draw for twenty years, I will make up for the lost time.

F: This is another kind of rationality.

H: In this regard, it is absolutely rational.

F: I think two factors made you draw like a madman. One was that fate owed you a lot. It was reasonable for you to seek justice in terms of time for your art. The other was your talent—infinite imagination, boundless thinking, explosive inspiration—which stemmed from your emotions and sensibility. Rationality and sensibility have jointly shaped your life.

H: Absolutely. In the past I had no choices in life, I had nothing, and I had to struggle hard for mere existence. To tell the truth, I had to paint to live. Wasn't that rational? But when I came out of Dongshan and back to the real world, I saw what I loved and started painting whatever I wanted. I was very sensitive to life and had a strong impulse to paint. Wasn't this emotion? What do you think?

F: You've hit the nail on the head. Let's talk about your paintings now. Do you attach great importance to a sense of wholeness and integrity? As far as I can see, whether it's a painting as big as a wall or as small as a stamp, they all have strong integrity. There's a sense of wholeness and they give out strong vibes. Do you put a premium on a sense of wholeness and integrity?

H: Of course, yes. A sense of wholeness is fundamental to a piece of work and I pay attention to it. Why are my paintings very striking? Because I am a Fine Art student. Mere technique is not enough. Paintings on their own cannot grab your attention. They require embellishment and this comes from strong colour and imagery. It's the first thing you see from a distance, this is extremely important. Picasso understood this. So, the first thing you see at a Picasso exhibition is 'Picasso'. It's also related to his study of Africa and pottery.

F: Your works are certainly extremely eye-catching. Is your symbolism related to this? Your works are immediately distinguishable from the work of other people. I don't want to use the concept of 'style'. Generally speaking, 'style' can be used for paintings. However, the important thing in your work is your use of symbolism.

Draft of ideas

H: Symbolism shows personality. I've just said that I studied Fine Art. Symbols are gradually refined from complexity to simplicity. Regardless of the shape or the colour, you have to be concise. It's hard for an artist to move from complexity to

FROM PURGATORY TO PARADISE

simplicity. It's a qualitative change. It's a milestone for an artist if they can do this.

F: Simplicity is harder than superfluities. But if you oversimplify you have nothing left and so you need to include even more. But if you want to simplify, you must destroy what you've already made, which is even harder, because it's difficult to destroy things that look good.

H: Moving from complexity to simplicity is like putting on a bet: it's not necessarily always a success and it can turn a somebody into a nobody. If you've a serious illness, you don't know if it'll be fatal or not but if you survive and lose weight then it enhances your spirit.

F: Have you had this sort of experience?

H: Oh, too many times. For example, wild grasses captivated me and some issues in my painting were solved at once with the drawing of these grasses. A few lines were enough. Of course, they weren't simple lines.

F: Do you think it's a kind of sublimation to change from complexity to simplicity?

H: More a kind of revolution. Let me show you a painting. This is a ballerina. Look at those brush strokes. There are no muscles, no expression and not much else. But there is the skeleton, belly and joints.

F: What's left when you have extreme simplicity?

H: What's left is the first impression—the most beautiful thing in this is the posture of the dancer. Here the skeleton, belly, joints are the vital parts for expressing this beauty.

AN INQUEST INTO THE KINGDOM OF ART

F: But not everyone thinks about simplification. Qi Baishi[3] thought about it so he made changes in his style in his old age. After this Qi Baishi entered a higher realm altogether.

H: Simplicity also requires a great deal of skill. Isn't composing five-character poems the hardest thing in literature for anybody to do? Solos are very difficult: monologues, solos, solo dances, storytelling, sketches, and so on. As well as these, a Capella singing, comic monologue, monodrama, storytelling, traditional delineation —why are they also very difficult?

F: Nothing accompanies them or helps them?

H: Yes, they need real skill. Let me give you a few more examples. What does simplification mean? Simplification means keeping to the key points. What does summarisation mean? It's about picking out all the important stuff. What does 'refining' mean? It's like smelting; like making steel from iron and glass by heating ordinary sand; like the traditional method of the Taoist Masters for making the pills of immortality. Chinese characters are certainly powerful. I think that Chinese characters can't be eradicated, and Chinese literature can't be obliterated.

F: Thank you for your thoughts on Chinese literature. Let's change the subject. Why are the images in your paintings dynamic rather than quiescent or static? I am not sure if my observation is correct or not?

H: You're right. Do you remember once asking me why I draw a horse but not the hooves?

F: Yes. You told me that if you draw the hooves, the horse stands still and loses any vibrancy.

H: In painting, paper isn't important, shape isn't important. For me, spirit is important, beauty is important, passion is important. Sensibility and perception are at the top of the list. What's the relationship between art and humans? Art is the culture of sublime people. Why is art a kind of enjoyment? Because one enjoys the essence of human beings and enjoys oneself. I have a clear character. I only look at things from a binary perspective: black and white, right and wrong, love and hate. I am passionate about these. I don't have time to mix things. I don't drink warm water—either I drink ice-cold water or scalding hot water. I hate lukewarm water. I'm deeply influenced by two sentences of a poem written by Li Qingzhao:

> Be a hero while alive and be the leader of the ghosts, even after death.

Once I was in Hengshan county in the Sanjiangyuan area and I saw that some folks were performing a *Qinqiang*[4], *The Death of Xiang Yu*. The person playing the part of the conqueror Xiang Yu was wearing a sleeveless costume with the cheapest makeup on his face. He had modelled a long nose and there he was, the conqueror Xiang Yu. He was singing vigorously and sweating profusely. His long hair was drooping down to his mouth. He raised one hand and stood like a pheasant on only one foot and jumped into the Wujiang river on one foot. Simply outstanding! I was so excited that I went up to him and gave him a thousand yuan.

AN INQUEST INTO THE KINGDOM OF ART

At that time one thousand yuan meant quite a lot. He kowtowed to me. He used to earn only 20 yuan a day. I was more excited than him because I liked the elements of strong folk culture.

F: Shall we return to my question—why are the images in your paintings so dynamic?

H: Because I'm dynamic, a jumping jack. I have discussed this earlier.

F: Is this related to your exuberance?

H: It's natural. I can't help it or control myself. You know this very well.

F: Here's another question. I am also very clear about it but would like to hear it from you directly.

H: Please go ahead.

F: In your works, which is more important, an aesthetic sense or their significance?

H: Beauty, of course. Aesthetic sense is cultural, a civilised life and a sublimation of the potential. Sublimation of the highest order.

F: Well said. Your concept of beauty is actually a kind of spirit.

H: Aesthetic perception can be realised, though.

F: This depends on the person. An aesthetic sense cannot be learnt or taught. Everyone must bring it into being themselves. We've talked a lot about the sensibility of your art. I'd

FROM PURGATORY TO PARADISE

now like to talk about the rational elements in your paintings. Do you start reasoning before you start painting? Or do you get a rational grasp of the content while you're painting? For example, Chinese literati painters always have a rational grasp during the process of creation, which is the pursuit of poetry and an artistic conception.

H: I start reasoning before I start painting. I'm more creative than rational. Art is the product of perception, not of reason. Of course, this perception shouldn't be taken for granted because rational thinking should be the artist's baseline. During the creative process, this should be sufficient for a baseline.

F: If it was more than that, would it be a restraint on you?

H: Yes. When you're creating art, you mustn't think of yourself or laws or methods. Many singers, conductors and actors have died on the stage; even Molière[5] died on stage during a performance.

F: Luo Yusheng, the famous artist was once performing on the stage using Beijing dialect with a drum accompaniment and she suddenly felt dizzy. The doctor was called and her blood pressure was found to be very high. She took some medicine and jumped back up onto the stage again. Later I asked her what she would've done if her blood pressure had continued to rise during the performance. She said that the show must go on and it didn't matter to her even if she died on stage. That's the trait of a true artist.

H: Xie Jin told me a very interesting story once. He said that some old actors couldn't remember long speeches and got

AN INQUEST INTO THE KINGDOM OF ART

nervous, and he knew about these feelings from when he was acting in a play. He got extremely excited and forgot his lines, but the camera was still running and shooting the scene. What should he do? He just shouted 1-2-3-4-5-6-7-8-9-10 with all the emotion needed by the storyline. The play was not interrupted, the filming was not interrupted and, after proper dubbing, it was indeed a good play. Art needs to express real feelings.

F: We'll talk more about sensibility later. I want to keep discussing rationality. The rationality you mentioned is about ideology, formality or technicality. There are various laws for creativity which you just said are based on technicality.

H: Most importantly, rationality is derived from your experiences in life, including travelling along the bumpy road of art. Rationality is a thread weaving through the soul of an artist. The form and technicality of art can't determine rationality. My rationality is conscience. Inwit conscience and a good heart aren't the same things. Inwit conscience is rationality; having a good heart is your basic nature. There are three different dimensions to Inwit conscience. One is to be a good person; this is extremely important. The second is the ability to survive— you must at the very least be able to support yourself. The third is to contribute to the world. Conscience is my rationality and my baseline as well. I've never separated being a good person from being an artist.

F: Who is your art for? For the many or the few? Do you want public recognition or recognition by a small group of people?

FROM PURGATORY TO PARADISE

H: While working, I never give any thought to it. I don't think about making lots, or a handful, of people happy. If people like it, I'm happy.

F: Some of your works are extremely large. We'll talk about your sculptures later for your city ones are enormous. If I refer specifically to your paintings, do you paint on a large scale because of an emotional need?

H: Huge paintings are my forte. Some important places, especially the National Palace, have invited me to paint works for them. These places are very large, and the walls are very tall, so the required pictures must also be very large. A hall in Venice was 11 metres long, so I had to do a painting of 11 metres. The National Museum has a 25-metre-long wall, so I did a painting of 22 metres.

F: It's been like this from ancient times both in China and abroad. Michelangelo painted the "Final Judgment" and the ceiling frescoes of the Vatican Sistine Chapel. Leonardo Da Vinci painted "The Last Supper" for Santa Maria delle Grazie. These paintings are very large and show the artists' forte. Daoxuan[6] also painted many large murals for temples in Chang'an and Luoyang. Big works are very difficult for an ordinary artist to paint.

H: I drew a horse in the Great Hall of the People. The head of the horse is one metre long and the buttocks are about one and a half metres. Do you know how big the brush was? How many kilos of ink I used? The ink would fall off the brush if I didn't work fast enough. The most important thing is that you must be passionate about it. It's different from oil painting. You can use small brushes for that. But the

AN INQUEST INTO THE KINGDOM OF ART

brushes for paintings in ink and colour can be bigger than mops. If you have no efficacy and not enough passion, then you won't be able to paint anything.

F: How big are the paintings you do in your studio?

H: Unless I'm working towards an exhibition, I paint only a few large ones, maximum four feet by six feet. That's just to please myself.

F: Where does your passion come from when you are painting humongous paintings? For example, while painting horses do you fantasise about galloping horses?

H: That alone isn't enough. Injustice, dreadful scumbags and horrible things—things that make you angry—come into your mind and affect your emotions. That's what makes you energetic.

F: So, all the vagaries of your life are combined in your paintings. I understand them better now.

H: Did you think, that to reflect life profoundly, I had to paint all the scum one by one? If I'd done that, I'm afraid it wouldn't have been art.

F: You are so passionate, enthusiastic and unconstrained; do you pay attention to every detail?

H: Didn't I make it very clear when I drew you the ballet dancing girl just now? Details are crucial.

F: Opera lovers have a 'niche' for opera; poets have a 'niche' for writing poems. For example, in the poem *Spring Breeze Once Again Sweeps Through the Green Jiangnan Field*, written

FROM PURGATORY TO PARADISE

by Wang Anshi, the word 'Green' can be portrayed as the most vivid poetic word. Do the painters have something special or a very salient point in their mind when they are painting?

H: Definitely. Without it a picture would be simply mediocre. Having a salient feature for painting helps with the minute aspects of the paintings.

F: In your freehand sketches it happens automatically, doesn't it?

H: It takes years of hard work before it comes automatically to anybody. If there's no hard work, there won't be any spark.

F: So, you don't plan the spark, you don't wait for it; it appears on its own. But it doesn't jump out without a reason. There must've been abundant accumulation and cultivation.

H: You've got it.

F: Now let's change the subject and talk about something else. There are so many images in your World of Art. Which are the most important to you?

H: All images are important to me. I draw them to satisfy my emotional needs. I love them all. I don't paint what I don't love.

F: So, all the paintings that you have made are all equally important to you.

H: Yes, all are equally important.

F: Even if some images are painted a bit more?

"Owl"

H: It doesn't matter. All of them are equally important to me.

F: Let's talk about a specific image—Lord Buddha. It's one of the most important in your works. Does it have any special significance for you? Is it a sign of your faith?

H: People must have faith whether they are religious or not. The Buddha epitomises 'goodness' to me. Be good to everybody; be kind to everything—including nature, including

FROM PURGATORY TO PARADISE

the smallest form of life, for example ants. They don't have an easy life. Everything that lives on this planet, no matter what kind of creature—big or small, old or young—doesn't find it easy to survive. We must stand at the height of the Buddha and look down until we see the smallest of souls—the little ants.

F: Speaking of ants, it reminds me of a childhood memory. Our house was opposite a sanatorium for workers. There was an old person there, a doorman, who was known as Mr Sun. He was a kind person and I liked him a lot. But one day I saw him standing there crushing something energetically. I didn't know what he was doing so I went closer and saw loads of ants had gathered round and were fighting among themselves. What about him then? What was he doing? He was crushing the ants one by one under the soles of his shoes, so the whole ground was as black as the Earl of Purgatory's waistcoat. The huge number of dead ants were like corpses on a battlefield. It made me sick and disgusted, and I never liked him again.

H: I agree. It was absolutely disgusting. Art does exactly the opposite.

F: In your works, including your sculptures and paintings, you can often find images of Lord Buddha. In your calligraphy too, you can see the sermons of the Buddha. I remember in the 1980s you wanted to carve the head of the Buddha on many Buddhist sculptures whose heads were lost. You're not a Buddhist. Did you do these things because you regard the Buddha as an idol of goodness, fraternity and compassion?

AN INQUEST INTO THE KINGDOM OF ART

H: Of course. Although Buddhism came from India and Nepal, and influenced Korea and Japan, its real development started in China. The three vehicles of Chinese art are palace and elitist art, Buddhist art and folk art. You can't find anything else except those three. Buddhism teaches us to be good and tolerant, doesn't it? So, I paint pictures of Lord Buddha.

F: The spirit is greater than the thought in your art. You focus more on spirit, and that's fine. We've already discussed this. The ultimate idea is spirit.

I now need to ask another question which is: "Do you pay attention to the social significance and value of your works?"

H: I haven't really thought about that. I enjoy being creative and being amidst art. I've suffered a lot and worked very hard as well. The Long March is over. It's time for the Red Army soldiers to have a mouth-watering meal of roast meat.

F: Do you like to create when you're enjoying something? I've seen that you often have music in your studio.

H: I like classical music: Mozart, Chopin, Dvorak, Schumann, Beethoven... there are so many. I also listen to American country music and I especially like folk songs. I paint whilst listening to music and sing when I'm happy. If you have music, every line you draw is enjoyable. Sometimes when the record or CD stops, my brain plays music on its own and I don't have to change the CD.

F: Do you prefer to paint after meticulous planning or without any planning at all?

FROM PURGATORY TO PARADISE

H: Without any planning.

F: In what sort of mood? When you're happy?

H: Not really. Happiness, anger, sorrow and joy—anything can inspire me.

F: You can still paint even if something unpleasant happens?

H: I'm not sure but perhaps I draw more zealously. My inspiration doesn't come from sweet things like beautiful flowers or applause from pretty women, but it comes from two words: shame and humiliation. Shame because of my own wrongdoing and humiliation because of insults from others. But I don't want to take revenge. I've said in the past: "Give me a block of iron and I will transform it into a motivational sculpture." Because what I pursue is to have a good character, be a good person and produce a good painting. Be a noble person not a petty person.

F: The spirit of your art is certainly very pure. I like it a lot. We've already talked about spirit as the core of your artistic world. Let's get some details now. Readers will also be interested in them. For example, are you very demanding about the materials and tools for painting or calligraphy?

H: I'm not very particular about materials; I'm quite adaptable. Perhaps it's because of my past experiences. You know my water brush painting was invented without rice paper. In fact, I like to try out new materials.

F: Would you feel uncomfortable if you were asked to use tools or materials you'd never used before?

H: Not at all. On the contrary, I'd be interested in trying them. Maybe something new and interesting would happen.

F: A new aesthetic! It seems that you've a very liberal aesthetic sense.

H: I make all kinds of brushes and materials myself. Look at these new brushes made from dog hair. I've a very good relationship with paper mills, including a Japanese one. They help me transform the paper and not only the colour. I also collaborate with the Shanghai Art Pigment Factory.

F: New tools and materials often bring new inspiration—a new aesthetic effect and a new aesthetic language. But some painters and calligraphers don't do this. Whenever they go to other places, they always take their own brushes with them. In this way, in their 'artistic language', not a single 'word' will change, and their paintings also won't change in style. Some people paint the same pictures all their lives with the same themes and the same images. They've stereotyped themselves.

H: I respect Wu Guanzhong[7] for this. He never replicated his paintings.

F: Wu once asked me: "Do you replicate your writings?" I said that I've written all my life and writing can't be repeated or it will be self-plagiarism. Wu Guanzhong said: "I never repeat. I don't know how to replicate." Why do people repeat? Repetition makes no sense.

H: I've never repeated myself.

FROM PURGATORY TO PARADISE

F: Of course not, because all your images and drawings jump out straight from your heart. When you paint a horse, there are always a thousand horses waiting behind.

H: If one horse is done, another will automatically jump into the mind.

F: The number of your works is simply enormous, and it's connected with the speed of your creation. I wonder why you work so quickly. Perhaps it's got something to do with your pursuit of simplicity. You're now at the extremity of simplicity, and you can eschew all the things you don't need. As you have said, only 'spirit' and 'beauty' remain. Perhaps that makes you paint more quickly. Also, your passion makes your brush run faster. Do you agree?

H: I've got a good memory and have a powerful ability to associate with many things. On top of that, I've been 'training like a devil' and I've accumulated a lot of experience over a long time. I feel like I'm no longer laying eggs like a bird but spreading spawn like a fish. If the belly of a fish is full of spawn, it spreads a lot of it as soon as you touch it. When it comes to accumulation, it's like clouds which have both Yin and Yang—water and electricity. The more they accumulate, the more vigorously it rains. Sometimes I feel like a storm.

F: I'm pleasantly surprised to note that you feel good about yourself. Now that you have some time and space, are there any genres that you are curious about, which make you want to get involved in them? What would you like to have a go at?

Exhibition at the National Art Museum of China in 1979

H: Oil painting. I tried that as soon as I had some spare time.

F: How did you feel?

H: I had a very strong feeling that it was something fresh.

F: So, do you have any new ideas? Anything completely different from the oil paintings of the past?

H: Yes, I've so much experience and I've thought about it for many years, and I think about it while doing other things. I've been holding on to the idea for years.

F: You've accumulated a lot of *esoteric* writings over the years, haven't you?

H: Yes, there's a lot and now they're spilling out of the bookcases.

FROM PURGATORY TO PARADISE

F: Have you ever felt depressed and dejected? Felt self-doubt or self-rejection? Recently I read a letter by Paul Gauguin written on the South Pacific island of Tahiti. The letter illustrates that he was distressed and in poor health. What was worse was that he thought his imaginative power and inspiration had dried up and he'd come to the end of a blind alley. Almost every artist has a similar phase of depression, particularly when they feel exhausted. Especially after the continuous use of one method, the aesthetic fatigue must make you extremely tired. You might even feel that you've come to the end of your creative ability, but that's not necessarily true. It might be the brewing of a new beginning. It's like hitting the wall in a marathon.

H: I've experienced that several times. But I didn't feel cold. I still had fire in my belly. I thought I couldn't paint in a similar fashion all the time. I wanted to find a new world. Then I started going down a new road like a 'caravan', down and down to find a new feeling.

F: What really inspires an artist is vibrant life. Life, whether folk life, historical life or natural life, is emotional, communicative and evocative. As for the 'caravan', we'll talk about that later. How did you get through your phase of depression?

H: I didn't go too deep into depression because I've been constantly renewing myself. Don't I always say that my 'golden era' hasn't arrived yet? I'm almost eighty. Now I can tell you it's almost here. That's because now an image comes to me by itself without me needing to run and find it. Now I paint freely as soon as I lift the brush. I draw without a plan

AN INQUEST INTO THE KINGDOM OF ART

and do it at my own pace. I must've reached that phase of life. I've accumulated a lifetime of understanding, preparation and experience.

F: Is there a specific time which suits you most for creation? Some people have a periodic cycle; others have their best phases linked to the seasons and nature. Pushkin's poetry flourished every autumn.

H: Yes, spring and autumn. During the flowering season of spring and then during the harvest season. Aside from these two seasons, monsoon days are also quite productive.

F: My most productive period for writing is summer. I hold the hot summer with one hand and write hard with the other. I have a special feeling. I'm a hard-working writer, and a writer in hard working conditions.

H: I paint all year round but, I don't know why, during autumn and spring I'm more enthusiastic, especially in autumn.

F: Does it worry you if someone stands next to you while you're painting?

H: Not at all, but I don't feel comfortable when people I don't like stand by my side.

F: Have there been any major turning points or major phases of change in your painting over the years?

H: As I said earlier, Helan mountains prehistoric art was a turning point for me.

153

FROM PURGATORY TO PARADISE

F: I'll ask questions about Helan mountain parietal rock paintings when we get on to the Yinchuan Han Meilin Museum of Art. Let me 'reply' on your behalf. Of course, my 'reply' cannot be considered as 'final', and you shall have to approve it.

I reckon 'esoteric writing' was an important turning point for you. Although it comes under the category of your calligraphy, it was never included in traditional calligraphy. It's an original creation of yours.

H: Yes.

F: Your calligraphy has been influenced by the Han dynasty[8], wooden tablets and Yan Zhenqing[9] and, although you have your own distinct style, it doesn't break away from the traditional line of calligraphy. However, since the beginning of this century, one can see a dramatic change in your calligraphy. First, the cursive writing which you researched for a very long time has turned into an excessively free style of cursive writing. Your cursive script includes both your traditional calligraphic skills and abstract painting. What's important is that your cursive writing suits your temperament, and from it you also get the pleasure of sprinkling happiness and liberation. From an aesthetic point of view, you blend your fluent cursive writing, ancient texts and brilliant painting very naturally and so your esoteric writing comes directly from paradise. After the exhibition at the National Museum, your esoteric writing received wide appreciation and acknowledgment from the art world. Since then, esoteric writing has entered Han Meilin's World of Art.

H: You're right.

F: Your esoteric writing suddenly made your paintings completely different from your earlier works. It made them simpler, liberated, with more imagery and formality. Am I right?

Exhibition tour to the USA in 1980

H: Yes. I was going to say that, but you beat me to it.

F: I've observed you both artistically and theoretically. Are you interested in theory?

H: Not really. Art is a practical experience for everybody. Different people have different experiences; it can't be imposed on anybody. You can get a reference from theory though.

F: An artist has two kinds of theories—one is quite methodical. For example, *The Art Theory* propounded by Auguste

FROM PURGATORY TO PARADISE

Roden. Among modern artists, Wassily Wassilyevich Kandinsky, Salavador Dali, Kazimir Severinovich Malevich and some others liked theory. Some old Chinese painters like Guo Xi, who is very famous for his text *The Lofty Message of Forest and Streams*, and Shi Tao, who is famous for *Friar Bitter-Melon on Painting* also believed in learning from theory. An artist's theory is different from that of a critic's. It's a summary of the artist's own theoretical thinking as well as his exploration of it in a systematic manner. In addition, artists have another theory of rhetorical essays and gossip. For example, Zheng Banqiao, Qi Baishi, your own *Narratives of Han Meilin*, and the Japanese artist Kaii Higashiyama's *Compilation of Dialogues,* are all full of emotion and have insight. They're all a way of gaining wisdom from a painter outside of his paintings. I really like to read them.

H: I love reading *Thoughts Beside the Ink-Stone.*

F: Written by Qian Songnie, wasn't it? In the book *Collection of Zheng Banqiao*, we can find lots of similar comments on painting. I reckon bamboo was the world of Zheng Banqiao: bamboo in the chest, bamboo in the hand and bamboo in the eyes, highly ingenious.

H: I like that. There's also: "Your skill is mature when you paint without a fixed style and new ideas keep emerging." How sublime!

F: I've only three questions left. First: why do you always say: "I haven't started yet"?

AN INQUEST INTO THE KINGDOM OF ART

H: I'm eighty years old now but I still feel like a child. I can be enlightened about any issue. I have attained enlightenment after enlightenment. Doesn't Buddhism talk about 'anatman'[10]? I'm gradually going in that direction: inactive, lawless, motionless, colourless, beyond any boundary and limitation—nothing matters to me, I'm thoroughly independent. But I feel my art will kick off again. Surely if you've lived life, it shouldn't have been in vain; there must be some more major accomplishments to come? That's why I always say: "I haven't started yet".

F: Second question then: "Which of your paintings would you say is most representative of your work?"

H: I don't have a ballot box, and I can't choose my own works. Whoever likes whatever work will make it my representative work.

F: Third question: "What inspires you the most? Is it happiness, stress, challenge, self-esteem or love?"

H: All of them. There's a line in the anthem *The Internationale* which goes: "There has never been any saviour in the world, we must save ourselves."

2
TRICOLOUR
ANCIENT, FOLK AND MODERN

F: Today I'd like to learn about the basic composition of your art. Your work is unique and exceptional. I want to know what the basic elements of it are. The reason I'm curious is that I can't find any evidence of any outside influences. It seems that Renaissance, Classicism, Baroque, Impressionism and so on have nothing to do with your art. I can't find elements of your work in the history of Chinese painting. All the established forms of art have had no impact on you. Did you intend to exclude them?

H: Let's put it this way: look at the famous paintings in Western churches of the 16th, 17th and 18th centuries. The images found there now look stereotyped. This shows that times have changed and the present situation is very different from the old days. Of course, you can't deny that art was great at that time but the first crab you eat doesn't necessarily mean it's the best crab. We can't always hide ourselves in history. The profession of an artist is one of individuality. He must be independent. I learnt all this in

TRICOLOUR

History of Art, but I can't remain a student and never finished my apprenticeship.

F: It seems you have a strong sense of independence. An artist must have such independent consciousness in the face of art history, so that he won't be frightened by it. Li Keran said: "Strike with the greatest effort and come out with the greatest courage." That's well said. But it's often hard to get out when you're already really immersed in it.

H: You can't get rid of it. It's contradictory.

F: Huang Zhou, the famous artist said to me that his calligraphy was: "Only to be appreciated and not to be copied". If you practice calligraphy after a model and you reach a level where your writing is identical to the model, then there is no way for you to get unleashed from that style. That's why Huang Zhou said he only appreciated others' works; he thought about the works of ancient people but vowed that he would never copy them and never become a kind of 'prisoner' of the ancient people.

H: When they're learning about their heritage and legacy, artists shouldn't forget themselves but maintain their dignity and individuality. They must keep on improving their own style.

F: Learn the language well, and then speak it openly with conviction. It seems that you seldom take anything from Chinese literati paintings as well.

H: Literati painting began during the Song dynasty[1] and was advocated by Su Dongpo or Su Shi. It was a revolution at the time. It removed the fetters of courtyard-style painting; and painters became free to paint what they wanted, and they could insert poetry. That was progress in the history of art. However, since later generations changed from respecting the ancients to worshiping them and following their traditions, literati painting became obtuse.

F: Following and repeating the same old route is a big problem for Chinese painting. A Russian friend once asked me: "Why do all your Chinese paintings look alike?" That's a fundamental question about Chinese painting. Coming back to you, you've neither fallen into the established forms of Western art nor has your own work become fossilised. So, what's the origin of your art? I have been observing you for a long time, I have researched you and I think there are two sources. The first one is ancient art. Would you agree?

Observing rock paintings

TRICOLOUR

H: Yes.

F: Do you agree that ancient art was rather liberal, free-wheeling and nebulous? It's still alive even today, unlike the established art forms which are all dead and stereotyped. Do you regard ancient art as your source?

H: Yes. The classics in the history of fine arts are as complicated as a hoop. Some people think it's a golden rule, a norm. I think it's a dead end. I've been going into this since I was at school. I had to get rid of this 'school thing'. I had to get away from it. I finally found my way in ancient art.

F: Did you deliberately pursue the path of this art or were you mesmerised by it?

H: First I was fascinated. Sensibility is very important to art.

F: If the things which you really like are there then it means that you become an integral part of that thing too. It is decided by your innate nature. The authenticity, simplicity, ruggedness, boldness and directness in ancient primitive art all match your innate nature. Therefore, although many artists like ancient things, they are irrelevant to their own art. You say: "Sensibility is very important to art" and that's an important statement. Innate nature is the decisive factor for artists and ancient art naturally becomes part of your 'art-genes'. So, I'd like to ask you this: there are different kinds of ancient art in different parts of the world, have you ever studied them? Do they resemble each other?

H: In ancient times, the art in various places was very similar. However, during the medieval period, we don't find such similarities.

Works related to rock paintings (1)

F: The deeper the culture, the greater the difference. During ancient times, inhabited places were widely scattered and there wouldn't have been any communication between them. But we do find a remarkable similarity in art. Pottery, for example, looks very similar in China, Western Asia, Ancient Rome and North Africa. Another example: hand carved rock paintings from thousands of years ago, which have been found in many parts of the world, also look similar. Why's that?

H: Not only in the whole world, but it was also like this even in our own country. For example, the old Chinese characters written in Henan, Guangdong or the Northeast are identical, even though they are thousands of miles away from each other and separated by mountains and rivers. People couldn't communicate with each other and it didn't really matter, so why are the characters for 'horse', 'tiger', 'dog'

TRICOLOUR

and 'pig' in the ancient writings all quite long and vertical, not horizontal? Why are they all the same? I can't understand it.

F: Perhaps it's the common nature of all mankind. Have you learnt from foreign ancient art?

H: Yes, I have. But even though I did, it didn't replace my own style. Different countries and regions have different natural environments, different cultures, different artistic techniques, different materials and even different forms. Learning is not for replacement, and this is my attitude.

F: The fact that you notice this shows you pay great attention to the national character of art. You consciously stand in the origins of a national culture. It seems you've maintained quite a rational view of ancient art. There's both an emotional view and a rational view. Sensibility comes from your innate nature; rationality from what you think about the national character of your art.

H: I ardently follow the saying: "Rational learning and maintaining a perceptual understanding of art". We should use reason to study and research ancient things and have a good knowledge of them, but we need our personal perception to understand art.

F: You said this very aptly.

H: What artists rely on is perception. Art comes from perception.

F: What do you think are the Chinese elements in ancient Chinese art?

163

H: Chinese elements were formed gradually and have been developing continuously. There have been changes and limitations during each era. The longer the history, the deeper will be the knowledge of the artists. But in the process every era has its limitations too. Neither Wang Xizhi[2] nor Huaisu[3] had seen Chinese bronze inscriptions[4]. The Mao Gong Ding[5] vessel was excavated during the reign of Emperor Daoguang[6].

F: And oracle bone inscriptions were discovered in 1899.

H: So, you can say that the Chinese elements are dynamic. In ancient times, Eastern and Western art had their own advantages and disadvantages, and you could say there was no fixed element. I think each had its own characteristics in that period, and these characteristics were their elementary substance.

F: Did you want to understand all these characteristics?

H: Of course. Without these specific characteristics, the art would not exist.

F: In ancient art, symbols and Chinese characters are extremely important. They are genuine ethnic symbols.

H: I've paid very detailed attention to these figures and symbols in my esoteric writing.

F: I've listed esoteric writing as a special topic to discuss later. So, let's move on. What do you think are the common threads between ancient and modern art? There are two points about this. The first is that your art is modern art. It has a strong sense of modernism. But it is very well integrated with ancient art and there must be a reason for this. The other point is that contemporary artists worldwide trace their sources to ancient art or primitive civilisations. Am I right?

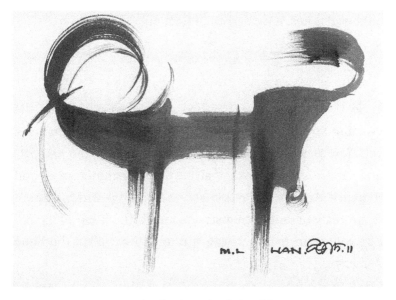

Works related to rock paintings (2)

H: Casualness. Ancient art has randomness.

F: Like the randomness of human life?

H: Yes. Human art had this only at the beginning and it isn't found later. When we produced an elite culture, there was no longer any such thing.

F: Apart from the randomness of the original, what else has made you integrate ancient art naturally into your 'World of Art'?

H: Non-commercialisation.

FROM PURGATORY TO PARADISE

F: You mean that primitive art was purely spiritual?

H: Yes. There was no guzzling and gulping of commodities then.

F: Apart from ancient times, what other eras, for example medieval times, have had an impact on you?

H: Any art before the Han dynasty has had a great influence on me.

F: So I've noticed. Han bamboo slips, bronze wares of the Warring States period and stone reliefs have all influenced you. You've not only learnt their shapes, figures and patterns but, more importantly, also their magnificence and romance. Art of the Han dynasty is quite romantic. It began to be realistic and nonabstract during the Tang dynasty[7]. But you seem to have little interest in art after the Song dynasty[8].

H: After the Song dynasty, it veered towards kitsch, so I have nothing to learn from it.

F: The main characteristic of the culture of the Song dynasty was 'marketisation' related to the rapid development of cities. Your art doesn't match. I think that only the shape of your porcelain, such as your bowl with a very small base, has some connection with the Song dynasty because porcelain making began then. The culture and art of the Ming and Qing dynasties[9] also have almost no connection with your World of Art.

H: You might say so.

166

TRICOLOUR

F: You have made a strong explanation about one of your sources—ancient art. What position and significance it has in your world of art, the essence of ancient art, and how much you value it!

You further talked about the relationship between ancient and modern art. Now let's talk about folk art. Do you agree that it has also inspired you?

H: Absolutely. I've already said that I'm continuing the work of rural artists.

F: From ancient times elite Chinese scholars have despised folk culture. Rural music and opera have been regarded as vulgar and folk art is not very refined. There are so many exquisite mural paintings in China, including the Dunhuang murals. Nobody knows who painted them because the painters couldn't sign their names. There are thousands of painters in the history of Chinese painting, but no particular painter is associated with folk art. Having said this though, there are two contemporary painters who are obviously related to folk art. One is Qi Baishi, who was born as a folk painter. His works were full of folk influence, but he finally ascended to the palace of the literati. The second is our own Han Meilin who studied at higher institutes of learning like the Central Academy of Fine Arts. Folk art flows in your blood and you promote the glory and spirit of it. Your sculpture, your themes, brushes, colour and materials all have a link to the common people. No elite painter in the history of China has ever loved folk art as much as you.

H: Yes, my veins are full of folk blood.

F: That succinctly expresses the relationship between your emotions and your folk spirit. This is extremely important. Let's talk about the essential difference between elite culture and folk culture. Over the past few years, I've been engaged in rescuing relics of folk culture and this has forced me to think about the essence and unique value of folk culture and its difference from elite culture. I think elite culture is created by individuals and reflects the height of the culture at the time. On the contrary, folk culture is created and recognised by people collectively and mainly represents the temperament, characteristics and spirit of a certain region and mirrors the diversity of the national culture. Elite art is a rational and conscious creation while folk art is an irrational and spontaneous life creation and directly represents people's spiritual ideals and emotions. Therefore, the two cultures have their own significance and one cannot replace the other. There's no question of which is higher, or which is lower.

H: So, the stone carvings in front of the tomb of Huo Qubing are no less great than the works of Picasso.

F: What do you think are the basics of folk art?

H: Even if their works are constrained by inherited procedures, technological processes, materials and purposes, they also follow their own nature and rules.

F: When they're based on the strict formulae of their ancestors, they appear stereotyped but when they're made according to their own personalities, they are often brilliant. Once I visited a woman in the Horinger grasslands in Inner Mongolia who was an expert in paper cutting. With the help of very big crow-like iron scissors she made me a 'fox' by cutting a piece of red paper. As she cut, she explained: "This is a female fox." When she was cutting the eyes, she said with a smile: "She's flirting." The fox's eyes were cut into a thin crescent-shaped hole, which certainly looked as if the fox was flirting. What was amazing to note was that only the eye was cut like a hole on the silhouetted fox. The simplicity and vividness were simply amazing. People who have this kind of ability are everywhere in rural areas.

Dyeing and weaving works

FROM PURGATORY TO PARADISE

H: It's just that they don't have a name and they can't sell their works for a high price. But real art has value not a high price.

F: Do you like the emotion in folk art?

H: Emotion is the most important thing in folk art. If there is passion, art is lethal. If there is no emotion, no amount of paint can bring life to the picture. If there is emotion, no force on earth can stop people liking it. If there is no emotion, even if you eat a lot of things, you can't become very healthy but if there is emotion and love, even God can't become an obstruction.

F: Real folk art isn't the folk-art performances at various beauty spots. Folk art is the emotional need of common people. Like ancient art, it originates from basic life itself.

H: Farmers have an extremely hard life and live in difficult conditions. When something good happens to them, they become very happy, put on colourful clothes, sing and dance, and are happy together. This is an expression of feeling and a living art.

F: You've talked about the innate nature of folk art. The theory of an intangible cultural heritage is known as 'living culture'. The point is that you have feelings for this living art. You treat it not as a form but as a kind of local beauty and an artistic object. You think of it as an emotion and so are often moved by it. What you've taken from folk-art is something beyond the art itself.

TRICOLOUR

Studying dyeing and weaving patterns with folk artists

Wood-carved chair

FROM PURGATORY TO PARADISE

H: You asked me once: "What have I learnt from folk art?" I've always been curious about everything in folk art. I learn everything from it. I learn from its sculpture, carving, painting, printing, weaving, archaeology, cutting, clothes, paper, grass, mud, stone, wood, everything. There are other sister arts like folk opera, dance, gongs and drums, folk songs, customs and colourful festivals. I like to dance, sing, knead, cut, tell stories, laugh and cry with them, but the most important thing I learn from them is how to be a good human being.

F: You put this very well. This is the soul.

H: In the past, the first thing you had to study about opera was how to become a good man.

F: You like the folk art of which region?

H: Why do you ask this question?

F: China is a big country with different topographies. The natural environment is different in different places and there are different customs and cultures, so folk art is also different. Over the years, we've discovered more than ten thousand types of folk culture and art in the country. For example, there are forty or fifty large and small areas of production of traditional New Year paintings, and the styles and themes are very different. Some are rough, some are delicate, some are simple, some quite complex. The folk culture of the Yellow River Valley is quite different from that of the Yangtze River Valley. Which one do you prefer ?

H: The Yellow River Valley.

F: Is that because you were born in Shandong? The Yellow river flows through Shandong, Shanxi, Henan, Shaanxi, Sichuan, Ningxia, Gansu, Qinghai and other places. The folk culture of these provinces is simple and rough, and quite different from that of the Yangtze River Basin.

We are a family

H: Some parts of the Yangtze River Basin are too delicate, to some extent a little artificial. Some are very secluded and beautiful, with a very different character.

F: Now let's get down to specifics. We're still talking about folk art, but we'll move on to things like colour. Why do you like rose red, jade green, yellow and purple as single and contrasting colours? Why do you use fewer composite colours? Is it because the main colours used in folk art are single and contrasting colours rather than composite ones?

H: Single and contrasting colours are the hardest to deal with. The most difficult part of painting is contrasting colours.

FROM PURGATORY TO PARADISE

F: That's because the art is simple. There are, however, only a few primary colours. If you can't express enough with these colours, the picture will be very simple. But folk artists are very knowledgeable—they always match the red colour with green, or yellow with purple, and this makes the paintings look very lively.

H: Many painters have studied foreign painting. They love foreign paintings but despise folk art. So, if you give them these primary colours, they don't know how to use them. Maybe they don't know that colour was used to express feelings in folk art.

F: It's a kind of culture. To understand it you have to assimilate yourself into the culture and be sensitive to it. Let's come back to you. Your art is modern art, but you use obvious folk elements in your art. Do you think modern art can be naturally integrated with folk art?

H: We've already talked about this.

F: Sorry. Let me put it in this way. Do you absorb folk elements from a modern standpoint, or do you paint modern art from a folk-art standpoint ?

H: They're complementary. But I started from ethnic and folk art. My position never wavers.

F: We've talked at length about the two inspirations of your art–ancient art and folk art. You haven't rigidly brought the ancient and folk-art forms into your World of Art, but integrated your art into these two sources and then created something modern. So, I sum up your art as ancient, folk and modern. I call these the three primary colours of your

174

art. No matter how colourful your art is, it has these three primary colours: red, yellow and blue. Do you agree?

H: Yes. They've shaped me. They've all had a huge influence on me and when I'm creating, they're my base.

F: When you're inspired by folk paintings, your work has a distinct sense of ancient times and a distinct feeling for modern times. When you do modern paintings, they also have a folk character and ancient connotations, so your art is ethnic, folk and Chinese.

Now let's move on to modern art. Do you think modern art can be divided into Eastern and Western? No one seems to care about that idea now.

H: Of course, it should be divided and, in fact, it's already divided.

Hard at work

FROM PURGATORY TO PARADISE

F: Why?

H: Let me give you an example about how you use a brush: in the West, such as in oil painting, you use it horizontally, drawing from the inside to the outside. In the East, that's not the case. In the East, you hold your brush upright and lift it up. Whether it's calligraphy or painting, the brush must be lifted up.

F: So that's why you said: "Already divided". There are a lot of basic differences between Chinese and Western art. But what I'm more interested in is your statement "should be divided", because nowadays very few people are interested in understanding this division. The East should have its own modern art and that should be different from the West, otherwise it seems that the modern aesthetics of art is the patent of the West. Whether consciously or unconsciously, or even subconsciously, everybody seems to be pursuing Western art. I think that's the fundamental problem faced by modern Chinese art. If we don't challenge it, we'll get to a dead end and die. You've solved the problem, but many artists haven't. I feel that our modern art–our contemporary art, has a sense of having been colonised.

H: I agree. Since the Opium War in 1840, China's momentum has rapidly declined, and the May Fourth Movement of 1919[10] made us knock everything down, even doubt everything.

F: And it mixed opposition to tradition with anti-feudalism.

H: Yes, it was an invisible cultural war. The May Fourth Movement was a double-edged sword. Most things have two aspects and it's difficult to avoid either of them.

F: Put your tradition aside before you clarify it. I didn't expect to taste this bitter fruit today, but I can't throw it away, and if I throw it away, then I'll have nothing left.

H: 'Subjugation to colonisation' that you mentioned continues today. "The giant underpants" as it is known–the CCTV building in Beijing, the Dashanzi Art Buildings in Beijing, the Round Art Community of Beijing—what do you say about these buildings? Can you find any Chinese elements in them?

Studying craftsmanship

F: Even if there are, they are simply ironic.

FROM PURGATORY TO PARADISE

H: This 'contemporary' thing is like the emperor's new clothes. Though only new clothes have a market value, the clothes of the emperor are not new creations. The market will then only pretend to understand. Therefore, this 'aesthetic' is not your own, not a new creation. You are deceiving yourself.

F: Therefore, there's no audience. Contemporary art doesn't match contemporary times, and this is probably the biggest crisis for the future of contemporary art. But now no one's thinking about the original point. Are modern aesthetics due to the difference between the East and the West? In other words, is there a global aesthetic? Is it the result of globalisation?

H: No, there can't be globalisation of art. Art emphasises individuality, independence and nationality. It's not a commodity. It can't follow the road of globalisation and internationalisation. There's no such path, just a ridiculous slogan. Globalisation of art sounds abnormal to me.

F: You've made your point. Now I'd like to know which modern Western artists interest you. Joan Miro, Salvador Dali, Wassily Kandinsky, Picasso, Henry Spencer Moore, Mondrian? Does the nationality of these artists matter to you?

H: We spoke at length about these painters earlier. They created their own unique forms in their times and the history of art should recognise their contribution. I once talked with a museum director in the United States about Marcel Duchamp's *Fountain*—a urinal signed by the artist. To this day *Fountain* is in a museum.

F: I saw it once in the Pompidou Museum of Modern Art in Paris. They'd borrowed it.

H: The director of the US museum said that they didn't praise him for acquiring it or say whether it was good or bad. They kept it just because it was a part of history and has significance for academic research. I think artists should respect each other. We should respect every important artist in history and distinguish between them.

Yuzhou city porcelain "Blossoming Mountain Flowers"

F: I agree with your word "distinguish". Modern science and technology can surpass previous innovations, but with art

FROM PURGATORY TO PARADISE

you can only distinguish between old and new creations. You're different from other artists and only then can your value be appreciated.

H: Exactly.

F: Were you influenced by Russian art and artists? Your generation was deeply influenced by Russian art. What's more, when you were in school, sketching was done according to the Chistyakov[11] system, and it was the time when Gerasimov and Maximov were teaching at the Central Academy of Fine Arts. Why weren't you influenced by them?

H: I was influenced by them, but I didn't take them at face value. I was influenced by them with regard to basic skills. You can see sturdiness in my work and there is not an iota of doubt that I got that from them. I thank Russian artists such as Surikov and Repin for their influence on me.

F: You already have your own system of practice; do you have any plans to establish your own specific theory of art?

H: Artists lay eggs and are not obliged to research the constituents and causes of eggs. Other people can do that.

F: What kind of art is your ultimate goal?

H: Still the same old words: "Not sure about it".

3
FOUR BROTHERS
PAINTING, ESOTERIC WRITING, SCULPTURE AND DESIGN

1: PAINTING

F: Today, we're going straight to your 'kingdom'. As I've said before I divide your World of Art into four fields: painting, esoteric writing, sculpture and design, and I call them "four brothers from one mother". So, let's talk about your four brothers one by one. First, painting. There are many kinds of paintings. Which kind of paintings do you paint most?

H: Traditional Chinese painting, marker-pen painting and painting drawn by hard-edged pen. Brush and fountain-pen paintings. In the 1970s, when I came out of prison and didn't have any painting implements, I invented my own way of painting with various tools. Now I only draw occasionally.

F: Do you call your painting traditional Chinese painting or ink colour painting ?

H: Chinese painting because it represents China or even the whole Orient. In the beginning so-called Chinese painting was related to characters and calligraphy. Initially, the brush emerged not for painting but for writing.

Painting

F: Therefore, Chinese painting, especially freehand brushwork, is not about painting, but about writing.

H: Oriental and occidental painting stems from two different cultures. As we've discussed earlier, when a Westerner takes a brush, it is called "holding the brush" and there is not much significance in this. When a Chinese takes the brush, it is called "lifting the brush" and we need to take a deep breath when we lift the brush. Chinese literati also combine calligraphy with spirituality - *Qi* and *Qigong*, - while Westerners don't have such practices.

F: Do you really care about these things?

FOUR BROTHERS

H: Take *Qi*. Without *Qi*, you can't draw a metre-long horse head. A huge horse and a big bull need to be painted in one breath. There is no such painting in the West. But in terms of tools, I hold that they provide service to me. For artists, tools and materials are never the most important things but thinking & imagination are the main driving forces. As long as the image comes from the mind, it doesn't matter what tools or methods are used.

F: I completely agree. Picasso used the handlebar and seat of a bicycle to complete his artwork *The Bull's Head*. Another example is Klimt who may have been inspired by Oriental inlay and ancient Roman mosaic works. He even used glass and gold foil on his canvases. It seems that you also attach great importance to image. "Image first", isn't it? Do you pay a lot of attention to the appearance of the image as well as what it is intended to express?

H: I focus on mannerism and form of the image and don't focus much on appearance. I deal with expression in separate stages. The first is sketching. Whenever I have the time, I go to sketch all kinds of facial expressions and emotions. For example, when I am overseas, I tuck a small notebook from the hotel in my pocket and whenever I get a chance, I take it out and make sketches of all kinds of distinctive faces and expressions. I've never stopped sketching. It's also an important part of my 'arduous-devil training' to figure out all kinds of expressions and emotions which I then use when I start drawing or painting.

F: I think you seem to pay less attention to the physical structure of the images but attach more importance to the combination of ink and colour. Your freehand brushwork is more and more succinct, even more abstract. I think you're refining yourself and reaching a higher level. Would you agree?

"Horse"

H: Yes, you're right. What you say about refinement is basically my continuous practice and it's been extremely difficult. You say I don't pay a lot of attention to physiological structure, that's true. However, I've practiced physiological structure millions of times. It's now familiar to me. It's my basic skill. No matter how I draw, the most important part won't be lost. Even if I draw just one line, it won't lose the most important aspect. Look at the bones and flesh in this line. They're all present.

FOUR BROTHERS

F: So, if you're so familiar with it you can easily do what you want?

H: Yes.

F: What are you aiming for now, then?

H: Image isn't a problem any more, now it's a matter of the beauty of brushwork and colour.

F: Aren't brushwork and colour formal things?

H: The formal sense of brushwork and colour is a kind of formal beauty, and it's a kind of self-accomplishment. However, it's also a kind of language. You must show the main essence of the image. If you can't show the main essence, even superb brushwork and colour are completely useless.

F: Brushwork and colour can't exist in isolation— this further reflects the fact that your painting isn't abstract.

H: Didn't Qi Baishi talk about "divine resemblance" and Li Keran[1] about "the importance of the soul"? Beauty of form must resemble divinity as well as the soul of the image. For example, if you paint four little swans dancing together and if one of them is shown bending its beak, even though it looks beautiful and has character, it won't be right. The four swans must have the same expression and smile together. If one is shown as bending its beak, you must change it. It's logical. Sometimes you paint with an absolute magical effect but to give an image of total beauty, you must cover up or even erase awkward expressions.

F: What do you think about the accidental beauty in free-hand brush work?

H: There's no such thing as chance in art. Some effects may seem to happen by chance but in fact they come out naturally because of many years of painstaking hard work. It's certainly not by accident or by chance. If there hadn't been several years of hard work, it wouldn't happen by luck.

Creating "The Eagle" for the Great Hall of the People, Beijing

F: So, you're saying that 'by accident' really means inevitable?

H: Accidents are sparks after a long period of hard work.

F: Another thing that I'm interested in in your paintings is colour. I mean the relationship between the ink and the colour. The primary medium in your painting is ink. Chinese ink is the primary feature of Chinese paintings. Yours is also Chinese ink-based paintings. It plays the leading role and is also the skeleton of your work. Then there is colour. The choice of colour is quite special; you rarely use traditional colours in your paintings, for example the golden yellow, jade green or light crimson colours used in traditional Chinese paintings. You use the colours which are primarily used in traditional folk art. Folk artists mainly use primary colours, which are extremely rich and vivid, such as rose red, emerald-green, lake blue, bright yellow. I don't understand how you combine the ink of traditional Chinese painting with the colour of folk art to form your unique colour system.

H: Black inkstick is the nucleus of Chinese painting and is unique to China. In Western paintings pure black inkstick is rarely used. Chinese ink itself is a type of language. A Chinese painting can be made without any other colours. The inkstick is enough. Chinese painters pay great attention to the value of ink and consider it as precious as gold. In fact, we cherish not only ink but also paper and colour which are also as valuable as gold. Chinese people have been trying to figure out how to put inkstick and other colours together for thousands of years. I think the most important experience for me has been to "cherish the colour". "Cherishing colour" means not destroying the language of the inkstick. Folk colours are just a few simple colours, but they are exquisite, and you must be very careful while using them. This kind of fastidiousness comes from poverty. Common people could only eat steamed bread and rice noodles several times a year. They would eat these things especially at New Year. To celebrate New Year, they would make a design on the steamed bread. You need to spend money to make it more colourful and buy red rose petals and emerald-green colours. You then have to heat them in a wine cup. After that you need to take a stick of grass and dip it in the colour to make a flower on the bread. It's incredibly simple but very colourful, very beautiful and very striking. Who wouldn't treasure these colours like gold?

"Fowl"

F: It seems you've very carefully put the colours of folk art into a framework of Chinese ink and really like doing it.

FOUR BROTHERS

H: It'd be an absolute shame not to. It's not easy to understand those colours and Chinese ink is even more difficult. Ink can be thick, light, dry or wet. Density and dryness blend colours and blending colours gives a grey tone. Black and white, red and green are primary colours and contrast with each other but they also rely on a grey tone to boost their brilliance.

F: Water also plays an important role in the intensity, dryness and wetness of the ink. You could call it the life of ink.

H: Isn't dry ink also very interesting? It's not easy to experiment only with black colour. When you talk about "water", you must also talk about the paper. Chinese paper is different from Western paper. Chinese paper absorbs ink and spreads it and makes the colour a bit greyish. You can do a lot of research on spreading colour on Chinese paper.

F: There are many more technical points about Chinese painting which we'll talk about later. I want to learn more about another kind of painting: painting with marker pen. This is unique, special, beautiful and extremely rich. You created it, didn't you?

H: I've used all kinds of tools for my paintings. For marker-pen painting I must thank the cartoonist Tian Yuan. In the mid-1970s I was still not rehabilitated and hadn't any brushes or Chinese paper. So, I was doing watercolours. At one time I lived in Tian Yuan's home in Nanjing. There were several marker pens on his desk. I hadn't seen those kinds of pens before. It felt good when I used them. My painting of *One Hundred Chickens* was painted in his house with a

FROM PURGATORY TO PARADISE

marker pen and later other people gave me some more of them. So, drawing with a marker pen gradually evolved.

F: Your marker pens have the wonderful effect of the movement of a brush on canvas. The edge of those pens is flat and square. The effect when they touch the paper is different. The key thing is that you're very good at experimenting with them and making the most out of them.

H: Difficulties aren't necessarily bad for an artist. Sometimes I use a marker pen in traditional Chinese painting, and it has a beautiful effect. Anyway, for me the image is supreme no matter what tools I use.

F: Your paintings of animals are lovely, friendly, and pure. Even fierce animals become tame in your paintings. Why?

H: I think that only when you've had an up-and-down life can you understand love. I didn't have any love in my life. No one sent me clothes in prison. Do you know how I survived from winter to winter with just a single pair of trousers, a single coat and a single rotten quilt? Only once a day when we were allowed to go out for exercise could we see the sky. When it rained, we could only hear the sound of the rain. When I was released and re-joined society, I had a kind of passion. I started loving everything in my life. I still do today. Now after dinner, I put the sesame seeds which are generally kept on the table into my mouth with my fingers. I often talk to nature and the animals that I draw. I think it has something to do with my experiences. The greatest love in the world is maternal love. I feel that I treat them with maternal love. No matter whether it's a snake, a fox or a bear, I regard them all as my children. It's that simple.

FOUR BROTHERS

F: Do you emphasise a theme in your paintings?

H: When I was young, I used to stress a theme. I couldn't understand a picture without a theme. Now I don't. Art has no single path, yet it also does have a single path. I draw what I love and whatever I love to draw, I draw.

F: The last question is about your sketch books. From your *Compiling Footsteps* called '*Nabu*' in Chinese in the Huainan porcelain factory until now, you've always carried a big or a small sketch book.

Draft of painting (1)

H: Yes. I've drawn in countless sketch books. I spend the most time drawing, followed by calligraphy, and pure painting ranks third.

F: What do you mainly draw in your sketch book? I think you must have images as numerous as huckleberries in these sketch books. I find that surprising.

FROM PURGATORY TO PARADISE

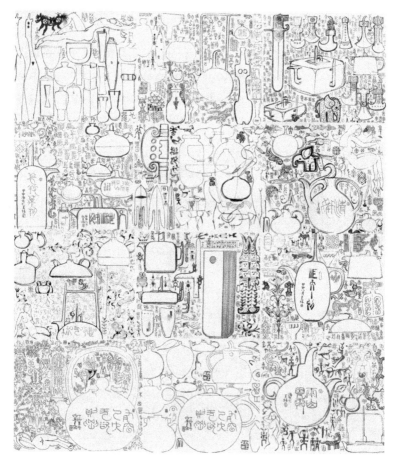

Draft of painting (2)

F: What was the original purpose of your 'devil training'? Was it just a part of your hands-on painting?

H: You're right. In the beginning, my self-esteem was taken away. In order to re-establish it, I was hard on myself and started rigorous 'devil training'. Now, to be honest, we are both accomplished in our own fields. Do we still need to paint or write so hard? We're both supervisors of several doctoral students so we need to have a good influence on them. We need real successors.

F: Do you enjoy yourself to the fullest when you draw these images?

H: In terms of creative work, I tell you, there is no enjoyment except hard work. I have to work extremely hard to create. Only after I begin to paint, that is after I step on the working table, then is it fun. The other purpose of my paintings is to make the audience happy. But before getting to the final stage, and relishing what I have accomplished, the previous work is a bit boring. I strictly separate these two aspects.

2: ESOTERIC WRITING

F: Let's talk about another big thing in your World of Art— esoteric writing. This is your way of doing calligraphy. I think that among your works, it is your esoteric writing that has attracted the most attention internationally. It has a strong sense of modernity and abstraction. Besides, in the eyes of Westerners there is a kind of Oriental mystery in esoteric writing. Occidental people always focus their attention and interest on the mystical aspect of the Orient. You didn't deliberately create the mystical aspect of esoteric writing because it is made up of ancient Chinese characters, an inherent aspect of our nation. Even though these ancient characters can't be deciphered, they contain the thoughts, spirit and ideas of ancient people. So, I believe your esoteric writing received international attention first but, of course, this creative modern calligraphy is also appreciated by our own Chinese people.

FROM PURGATORY TO PARADISE

H: That's right. For next year's Venice exhibition, the organisers have suggested that I use esoteric writing and rock painting to "move the world".

F: In their eyes it's a unique and pure art: abstract, modern and oriental, something which they don't have. The point is that there's a deep history and culture behind it. Can I dissect the origin of your interest in it? When did you learn calligraphy? Whose calligraphy were you most interested in? Who did you learn from? What method was used?

H: When I was just a few years old, during the winter and summer recesses at primary school, to prevent me getting into mischief at home, I was sent to a private school to learn basic writing. In the beginning, I studied the calligraphy of Yan Zhenqing[2] and after that I learnt the work of Liu Gongquan[3]. My teacher thought I had a tough personality, so he asked me to concentrate on the style of Yan Zhenqing.

F: Do you think that the style of Yan Zhenqing suited you more?

H: I gradually learnt about him. He'd been an official and was strangled fighting for justice, so I highly respect him. I also realised that there is a sort of righteousness in his calligraphy.

F: Righteous people are solid like iron and their works are also like their own personality. This is the tradition of Chinese calligraphy. At the very beginning did you learn by tracing in black ink over characters printed in red?

FOUR BROTHERS

Working on esoteric writing

H: We had to show it to the teacher. If it wasn't well written, the teacher would hit us on the palms of our hands with a long stick. Our fingers used to get swollen. Even if we couldn't hold the brush, we still had to write. That's the way my childhood skill was honed.

F: I can see elements of Han bamboo slips in your calligraphy. What do you like about these slips?

H: Han bamboo slips are like beautiful people. Look in this notebook at these Chinese characters for "Wu" meaning "Void". How beautiful they are! They are also so different from each other. Each character is beautiful.

F: Yes, dignified and elegant with a mystic aura. I especially like the long, vertical and horizontal lines of these bamboo slips.

FROM PURGATORY TO PARADISE

H: Yes, having said so, writing the character 'Fang' is not so easy because of all the different strokes this character has. It's a bit difficult to write and you need to be very careful.

F: Yes, I can see. Your skills of writing Yan calligraphy and Han bamboo slips are all integrated into your esoteric writing.

H: Also, *Kuangcao* — a highly cursive script. I've practiced this kind of cursive writing a lot.

F: The thing is that behind all cursive writing there are dense cultural and aesthetic connotations which you had to incorporate into your *esoteric* writing. If you do not incorporate these things, then it loses its essence and doesn't carry the same aesthetic weight. Another important element is classical Chinese characters. As we discussed earlier, in the 1970s when you came out of prison, you started to research ancient Chinese characters and got books from the Shanghai second-hand bookstore, such as the *Six Books* and the *Collection of Chinese Bronze Inscriptions*. It seems that you've a great interest in rock paintings, bronze inscriptions, oracle bone inscriptions, and characters and figures inscribed on stone tablets which haven't yet been deciphered.

H: Yes. You see these notebooks beside me. I've not thrown a single one of them away. I've always kept them intact and treasured them as my notebooks of calligraphy.

F: Are all the ancient characters in your esoteric writing undecipherable? Are there any sources?

196

FOUR BROTHERS

Samples of esoteric writing

H: Of course, all of them have origins. Do you think I have such a big brain? Can I create so many mystic characters? Can I just casually invent some characters? I daren't draw a stroke without a source. You may think I write these characters casually but in reality, the font is based totally on that of ancient people. If I was able to create these characters, how could they be called "esoteric characters coming from Paradise"? I've collected thousands and thousands of characters but drawn only a very small number of them.

F: Do you consider this kind of symbolic ancient writing to be a different kind of painting?

H: Originally ancient people drew these kinds of pictures to record events. Some of those graphics gradually evolved into Chinese characters.

FROM PURGATORY TO PARADISE

F: It's said that calligraphy and painting have the same roots and started at the time of Zhao Mengfu[4]. But it seems that it started in ancient times.

H: It all started in ancient times. Not painting, that is, but the characters. In ancient times, when drawing a picture of five foxes for example, people would make five symbols. Is it literature or is it drawing? What happened to Zhao Mengfu at that time?

F: When did you start drawing esoteric characters?

H: Not in the beginning, it was very casual. At first, I just felt that ancient characters were so beautiful, and I couldn't differentiate between a painting and a character. Palaeographers didn't do much research on them and calligraphers didn't pay much attention to them either. So I thought why shouldn't I do something about them? They are all the creation of our ancestors; they are all beautiful things from our past. Apart from that, I must also thank Qi Gong.[5] He once saw me collecting all those ancient characters which nobody could decipher. He told me how beautiful they were and that it would be an absolute shame if nobody worked on them. He then went on to say: "You're an artist. Your calligraphy is at a fantastic level. Why don't you write down those precious characters?" His encouragement was a great motivation for me.

F: When you started writing esoteric characters, they were fantastic, and you used an ancient way of writing, like seal script.[6] You also used Han bamboo strips and sometimes even a bit of rock painting. Your book *Esoteric Writing*, which was published in 2008, contained these. Gradually you used cursive script and then extreme cursive script. Extreme cursive script matched your personality. The inner beauty of ancient characters was revealed, and so your personality was displayed as well. In that way you entered a new realm. The first time you really displayed it in public was the Han Meilin art exhibition at the National Museum.

H: Of course. Also, the cursive writing.

F: And by that time, your esoteric writing was already mature, and you were widely recognised and appreciated by the art community. Some people regard your esoteric writing as modern calligraphy because it has a strong sense of modernity.

H: Of course. I'm a modern man so how can I not have a sense of modernity?

F: Some people think that your esoteric writing is abstract painting. Would you agree?

H: I'm fine with whatever way you want to look at it. Everyone has their own way of looking at and appreciating it.

F: Has esoteric writing had any impact on your painting? I know that your bamboo *strips* of *Prajñāpāramitā Sutra*[7] have become open-minded.

H: There was certainly a mutual influence.

F: On the form or on the lines of your paintings?

H: The aesthetic of the lines of esoteric writing has been integrated into my painting. It wasn't intentional; it just

FROM PURGATORY TO PARADISE

happened. But there's another point: I delved into esoteric writing from the perspective of art. I paid attention to form. I was excited by the abstract image of esoteric writing. From this point of view, esoteric writing is both calligraphy and painting.

3: SCULPTURE

F: You've a background in the graphic arts so when did you become interested in sculpture? Was it at Huainan Porcelain Factory? You've told us earlier that you often moulded animal sculptures for friends and workers, and added colour and that they all liked them.

H: It was much earlier than that. When I joined the army in 1949 as a junior staff member in charge of communications, the commander saw that I liked painting. When he was transferred to the Jinan Municipal Committee to build towers, he took me with him. He built a memorial tower for the martyrs. There were reliefs on it. Several painters worked on the reliefs with carbon-iron bars and this is how I came to be in touch with sculpture.

F: Are you possessive of space?

H: All spaces are spaces for art for an artist. When you see a space, as an artist you naturally think of putting a piece of art there. It generates an automatic artistic feeling.

F: There is also imagination of the art. Western sculpture attaches importance to anatomy whilst Chinese sculpture attaches importance to vivacity. Which side are you on?

FOUR BROTHERS

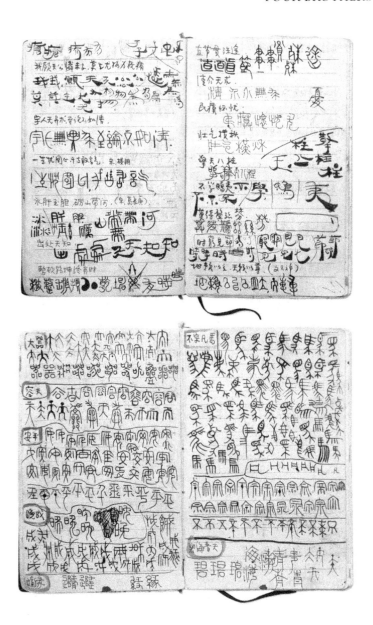

Collection of manuscripts of ancient texts (top, bottom)

H: I'm inclined towards vivacity, but human anatomy is my basic skill. I've mastered the structure and proportion of the human body. But the key is to learn the vividness of Chinese sculpture. For example, the 28-metre-tall sculpture of Guan Gong[8], which I designed, and which has been erected in Jingzhou, Hubei province. I don't regard it as a deified historical figure; I regard it as a symbol of justice—a mountain and a fierce wind. Sculpture must have a sense of mystery.

Working on a sculpture

F: This mystery has deep connotations which can't be understood by just a cursory glance.

H: No matter how big you are, how enormous your work is, you still need people to see it and understand it properly.

F: The larger the work, the larger the inner aspect becomes. I know you like the sculptures and grottoes of the Northern Wei dynasty in Yungang very much. Why? Apart from what people often say about the solemn and dignified atmosphere, what else attracts you?

H: What I just said—the mystery. I stood in front of them and felt puzzled. Also, there are the statues of the Northern Qi dynasty[9] in Qingzhou, with thin clothes closely fitting the body, which are extremely beautiful. Who says Chinese people don't understand human anatomy? I may not understand medical anatomy, but I can still find several important things in the human body.

F: I once asked Qian Shaowu[10] what he thought of the thinly clad figures of the Northern Qi dynasty. That style didn't exist before the Northern Qi dynasty and didn't even appear during the subsequent Northern Zhou dynasty[11]. Qian said it was influenced by Central Asian art. That gave me food for thought. There's an ancient Chinese saying: "How gorgeous the works of Cao are, as if water is flowing from the sculptures, and how splendid are the works of Wu, as if the clothes of the figures are being blown by the air." Cao's works and figures are 'slim-fit' sculptures with scanty clothes and he's from Central Asia.

H: I'm surprised to hear about the works of the Three-Star Mound[12]. How could they be so intrepid, so fierce? Why are we so timid? Can we dare to be as bold?

F: Unlike science, the history of art does not necessarily evolve and progress day after day. In ancient times people's material resources were limited but the space for spiritualism and imagination was much larger.

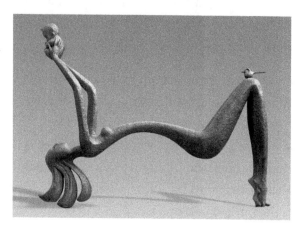

"Mother and Son" sculpture

H: Artists don't live a material life; they live a spiritual one.

F: Let's talk about your city sculptures. They are enormous, often tens of metres tall. In the last three decades China has entered an era of big sculpture. In the extremely rapid development of our cities, and in the unprecedented building of infrastructure, there has been a need for new symbols. The construction of urban sculptures has emerged, and this is also related to the showcasing of the political achievements of government mandarins. It's been a boom period for the creation of large-scale sculptures. Your masterpieces have been erected in many cities all over China. From the sculpture of roaring tigers at the Laohutan Scenic Attraction site near a beach in Dalian to the newly completed Guan Gong in Jingzhou, Wuhan, Hubei province, they are all huge. Do you think our cities need such large sculptures?

H: How tall are the buildings in our cities now? It was impossible to build so high in the past. The city skyline of old Beijing was flat. It was perhaps only around ten metres high. In the past, we could see a figure of the Buddha only in the mountains because it needed high mountain ranges. A few years ago, the Shanghai Park International Hotel only had 24 floors and it was the pride of that city. A building of 24 floors means nothing now. Urban development has forced us to make bigger sculptures. These are landmark sculptures, and if they can't be seen by people, how can they be called a symbol of the city?

F: That's logical. For example, La Grande Arche de la Défense is much larger than the Arc de Triomphe de l' Étoile in Paris. It has become a symbol of modern Paris. What kind of feeling do you want to give people through these enormous works? Pride, high-mindedness, self-respect and awe for their city?

H: Everything. For example, through the sculpture 'King Qian Lu shooting the tidal bore' which I designed, and which was erected at Qiantang river in Hangzhou, I wanted to show people's historical yearning for peace. Therefore, in my sculpture I depicted the story of King Qian Wu shooting the tidal bore and protecting the local community, and promoting this urban spirit. And take the sculpture at Daqing. There was absolutely nothing there. It was a wasteland. Generations of people have been engaged in producing oil from the fields of Daqing. I designed a mystical fiery phoenix to show the place rising step by step. Isn't that the pride of the people there?

Working on a city sculpture

F: Which of your city sculptures are you most proud of?

H: All my works are like my own children and so it's hard to say which one makes me the proudest. But 'Safeguarding Peace' which I created for UNESCO is my favourite work.

F: I really like the sculpture '*Sailing Through the Five Clouds*'[13] you created at Baiyunshan airport in Guangzhou. It's surreal and ethereal. You get the same kind of feeling of flying as when a plane takes off. Dynamism is a characteristic of your sculpture and, in fact, of all your art. All your works are extremely lively and permeated with a strong sense of vibrancy. Vibrant art can be infectious and influence others. Another question. Many of your sculptures, especially the bronze ones, evidently draw inspiration from the bronze wares of the Warring States period.[14] Do you like these?

"Deer" (left) and sculpture at Shenzhen stock exchange called "Lucky Dragon Bringing Fortune to Earth from Heaven" (right)

H: Things in the Warring States period were very rigorous. From the Xia and Shang Dynasties to that period there was still a slave society. Bronze mirrored the wealth, prosperity, power and even massacre of the masses. So, it was a stately, dignified, strict, strong and sublime period.

F: And to some extent domineering. During the Han dynasty, there was still the same trend, but it became a bit more romantic and relaxed. At that time there was no ritual human sacrifice during the burial of the dead. Instead, they used terracotta figures as symbols to show that society had progressed.

FROM PURGATORY TO PARADISE

H: And during the Tang dynasty things became even more so, didn't they?

F: Art became more figurative. How do you use things from the bronze wares of the Warring States period in your art? For their systematic value and rigorousness?

H: I can answer in one word — "Refining".

F: Refining in the smelting furnace of your personality? That's very difficult. It requires a strong personality, as well as the ability to juxtapose cultural tolerance and ablation. Finally, one more question on sculpture. Most of your sculptures are related to maternal love, women and babies. Why?

H: My bottom line is love, love and love. I also have many animal sculptures.

F: Are they sort of an extension of your animal paintings?

H: Of course. Animals can't speak and many species are dying out. The Japanese ibis is from the same species as the Chinese ibis. A few years ago, only nine Japanese ibis were left. I drew one and called it *The Tenth Ibis.* Now the Japanese ibis has become extinct. It's human beings who have stolen animal spaces. Of course, I will speak for them, show their beauty and arouse people's love for them. Stephen Hawking said that if human beings steal the earth in this way, the earth will be destroyed in five hundred years, or a thousand years at the most.

FOUR BROTHERS

4: DESIGN

F: Design is only one of the four brothers in your World of Art, but it seems to be the most important. It's ubiquitous. There are elements of design in your paintings, books and sculptures. Because of it, your art has a strong sense of form and impact; it makes your images more integrated and your world more independent. Other painters hardly know the art of design. There's no element of design in traditional Chinese painting. Among Western painters, there are not many with a good sense of design. Henri Matisse and Picasso had a good sense of it and so had the Austrian painter Klimt whom we discussed earlier. So, we must talk about your design. You are from the Central Academy of Arts and Crafts and have been engaged in Fine Art and teaching Fine Art and decoration. You're a professional, sensitive, and familiar with embellishment and decoration. Even now design plays a large part in your artistic creation. Your design can be divided into two parts: first, 'modelling design', which is reflected in your ceramics, glassware, woodcarving and Yixing clay pots[15]. Second is 'pattern design', which is mainly reflected in dyeing and weaving, the patterns of utensils and your logo designs. Many of your logos are famous, such as the Air China logo. All your designs have their own stylish colours. It's not easy to do. Did you pursue it deliberately? Or was it accidental?

H: Art is natural. You just do your work with all your heart. It's done according to your temperament. You form your own style; you can't copy someone else's. Pretension is not style. I must emphasise that my efforts at design have been

209

FROM PURGATORY TO PARADISE

very great and I have spent much more time on design than painting.

F: What you do you want to show through your designs?

H: Design is different from painting. It's not to show yourself, but to understand each other. If you're invited to design for foreigners, you should know first what kind of flowers their country likes and which colours they don't like.

F: Do you have a favourite colour?

H: Yes, I have some favourite colours for paintings, but you can't have one for design. Colour is like oil, salt, soy sauce and vinegar. The designer is like a master chef. When you're cooking, if you want the food to be salty, you put in some salt; if you want it sour, you put in some vinegar; if you want it hot, you add chili. You must treat colours equally. Whatever you want, you must use.

F: What's your philosophy of design?

H: There are two aspects. One is beauty. You need to learn a lot about this. But it needs to be practical. For example, see this pot. The handle can't be too thin, or it'll be easy to break it, and the spout can't be too low. If it's too low, you must put less water in. Also, you need to know how to make the materials. If you don't know how to make the materials, you won't be able to make the finished product. If you do know how to make them, you will be able to do the design full justice.

FOUR BROTHERS

Icons for the 2008 Beijing Olympics (top) and 'Fuwa' (lucky dolls) as mascots of the 2008 Beijing Olympics (bottom)

211

FROM PURGATORY TO PARADISE

F: So, you're talking about two integrations of design—practicality and materials.

H: Yes, those are the basics. With those prerequisites, you can talk about the issue of beauty.

F: If you consider your woodcarving 'chair', you've adopted a lot of ancient and folk elements in both your modelling and your designs in relief. There are elements from royal classical, Dunhuang art, pure folk art. Do you also include ethnic elements in your designs?

Air China logo

H: You may not have noticed but I've incorporated some elements from Africa, Latin America, Australian Aborigines and even Southeast Asia. I'm open-minded in design. It's different from painting. Of course, being open-minded doesn't mean opening up completely to the outside world. My work's mainly national because our national resources are so rich.

F: Two more questions. First, do you use your emotions in your designs?

H: All kinds of art are perceptual in the first place. However, there are some exceptions with design. My painting and esoteric writing are more perceptual, my design is mainly rational.

F: The second question. Decorative art is more oriented towards the outside world. Do your other three brothers as you call them—painting, calligraphy, and sculpture - have a powerful impact because they have elements of design?

Busy with design work

H: Yes. Decorative art is for others to see, unlike painting and calligraphy which are for oneself. Only when you want people to see your designs, will they pay attention to you. Design makes me care about other people's feelings.

F: That gives your art a wide audience. It isn't targeted at a minority. Through this conversation, I've learnt many important things about the theory of contemporary art. I think they are of huge significance and have great value for research.

4
ONE MAN'S MOGAO CAVES

F: We've been discussing your life and works for more than two years. Do you remember that it was during the Two Sessions[1] in 2014 where we talked every night in a room on the top floor of a Beijing hotel? Since then, there have been many interruptions as either you or I have been extremely busy. But this year I made up my mind to finish the project in one go. Now it's almost completed, and an idea has come into my mind—to do a summary of the whole project. I thought it would be difficult, but I've had a sudden inspiration: I've realised that your three art galleries are the best summary of your life and works. Isn't it a fact that your World of Art is kept in these galleries? So, let's talk about them. Few artists in the world have three galleries, let alone ones as large as yours. In terms of scale, category and quantity, these are so huge that during the inaugural ceremony of your Beijing gallery, I said that this is your "one man's Mogao Caves". Why did you want to build museums in Hangzhou, Beijing and Yinchuan? Do they differ in content?

ONE MAN'S MOGAO CAVES

H: The Hangzhou *Pavilion* is quite comprehensive. My so called "Four Brothers" are all there. The Beijing *Pavilion* is the largest with a huge number of works and is not only comprehensive but also classic. New works are constantly added to it. Yinchuan is unique as it shows the connection between me and the source of Chinese art, and my relationship with these roots.

F: It also shows respect for tradition because you've an extraordinary relationship with rock painting. The significance of these museums is the respect of contemporary Chinese artists for their own culture. They also showcase the continuous flow of Chinese civilisation to this day. How large are your museums? Do the displays change regularly?

H: The Beijing Pavilion is now approximately 13,000 square metres and will be further expanded to 29,000 square metres next year. The Hangzhou Pavilion is about 6,000 square metres. The Yinchuan Museum is around 7,000 square metres and is currently being expanded. The works are changed every five years, though there are usually only minor changes.

F: Is the continuous expansion and replenishment of content related to your continuous exuberant creating?

H: My vigorous creativity is an objective existence; I'm unable to stop myself.

F: Some people have termed your creativity a 'total blowout', but I prefer to call it a 'nuclear fission'. Some of our friends have found it a bit strange. Why are you still so creative at your age? Mo Yan and Liu Shikun[2] have jokingly

215

FROM PURGATORY TO PARADISE

said that someone should carry out scientific research on your brain.

H: A painter enriches himself after accumulating years of experience. The older he is, the richer in experience he becomes. There's some sort of organic relationship between his age and his experience.

F: Let's change the topic. Art auctions are one of the ways to advertise one's art. Why do you insist on not entering the auction market? What are the disadvantages when your works are sold at auction?

H: I can only make progress when I don't need to compete against anyone. The auction market traps artists. I won't let anything kidnap me. As I said before, the emphasis in art is on value, not on price. As long as I can live my life fully, things other than art don't matter much to me. I've already decided that when I leave this mundane existence, I'll tell three jokes to say goodbye to my friends and the world. That's my outlook on life.

F: There are two other things I'm curious about. One is your so-called 'caravan' and the other is your public welfare activities. Is your 'caravan' the main way for you to get connected with people and history? By 'history' I mean historical and cultural spaces, such as the Helan mountains, Yungang grottoes, the cultural relics of the Dazhao temple and the sites of Western civilisations. Civilisation started with the common people in the countryside not in the big cities.

ONE MAN'S MOGAO CAVES

The Beijing Pavilion (top), Hangzhou Pavilion (middle) and Yinchuan Pavilion (bottom)

H: I can't do without being in touch with the grassroots of society. Without a grounding in them, I have no confidence to create. This year I've already been to hundreds of places.

FROM PURGATORY TO PARADISE

Two days ago, the Canadian government invited my "caravan" to make aboriginal totem poles.

F: I know that your caravan is not a car or vehicle but the name of your crusade for collecting cultural items so why do you call it a 'caravan'?

H: I got the name from a film made in India[3]. In it was a group of vagabond actors who went from place to place and wherever they found somewhere suitable, they performed there. We do the same. I often go to the countryside to do research for my works including dyeing and weaving, pottery and glass products, and I talk with the folk artists and learn their skills. Folk artists know so many powerful things and one can learn a lot from them.

F: Where does your immense feeling for folk art actually come from?

H: From my sufferings. Without suffering, how could I understand them? Without pain, how could I be in touch with them? I love them a lot.

F: My next question is about your "welfare foundation". You have undertaken so many benevolent public works. What makes you do these things?

H: I'm determined to support deprived poor people, especially poor folk artists. But I must send my support to the artists, to the students directly and not through any official channel.

F: Finally, I have two more questions to finish off our conversation. Zhou Jianping, your wife, came into your life late but is the most important person to you. You and I have been friends for more than three decades, so I know what she means to you. She is your companion, the home of your emotions and the real devotee of your career. She appeared on the horizon just as your World of Art was about to expand. Your three art galleries have been shaped meticulously by her own hands. She has taken on all kinds of things and a multitude of pressures both inside and outside your home. But, when you are in public, one seldom sees even the shadow of Jianping.

Mountains of drawings piled up in the studio

H: No, she doesn't participate.

F: But she's everywhere in your world – that's the role of a wife. For a husband, a wife is omnipresent. She is a woman of high calibre. Let's talk about the meaning of the wonderful word "Wife".

FROM PURGATORY TO PARADISE

H: OK, let me proudly and immodestly say that my wife is my number one. She gives me the maximum support when I'm devoted to my work.

Han with his wife Zhou Jianping

At the art exhibition held at the National Expo

ONE MAN'S MOGAO CAVES

F: Well, you're honest and direct in your reply. You said: "Number one" and that says everything. This is just your style – direct and reflecting your sentiments. Your friends all know how much it takes to satisfy the needs of a super-improvisational, wilful and hyper-active person like you. Now let me ask the last question.

Assessing your whole life, it could be said that God owes you a debt as you had to suffer so much during the first half of your life. God paid you back as in the latter half of your life he let you do the art works you are so obsessed with. He also gave you a very capable assistant and a partner who completely understands you. You're now 80 years old and extremely energetic, quick witted and smart. When we talk about the word "destiny", the meaning of the word is very deep, sublime and wonderful.

H: A human being needs to acknowledge destiny. My life is divine and strange, but I'm not stupid.

1 August 2016

APPENDIX

IN PRAISE OF HAN MEILIN

1.

IN CURRENT ARTISTIC CIRCLES, the only person who consistently amazes me every time I see him is Han Meilin.

Yesterday, I was overwhelmed by the completely new artistic vocabulary that he has developed; today, he has turned his studio into a visual world that none of us have ever seen before.

He has constantly changed himself—recreating himself in the blink of an eye. Every day he is saying goodbye to yesterday; every day is begun completely afresh. However, a true genius can seem to be spurred on by the gods to unexpected and amazing ends, which not only shock others but also often surprise themselves. Whenever this happened, he would phone me: "Come to my studio as quickly as you can! You've got to see my latest painting, it's really great!" He

APPENDIX

would look forward to sharing this moment with his family and friends. When I stood in front of his painting, unable to stop myself from expressing my admiration, he would then say: "Believe it or not, I haven't even started yet!"

I love it when Han says that.

At that moment in time, I can sense a kind of invisible, majestic creativity burgeoning in his mind. It is like a volcano spewing out ash prior to an eruption. This is the most wonderful feeling that any artist can experience—and the most mysterious.

2.

How great is Han Meilin's creative imagination? That is a mystery.

For more than 20 years, I have kept a close eye on him. The whole time I have been dazzled, to the point where I can no longer sense the horizon or the direction of travel. At one time, it was all rough and heavy bronzes, then it was smooth, colourful ceramics; after that he was making stone sculptures over ten metres tall, then tens of metres tall, and then mountainous sky-scraping statuary hundreds of metres high; then, all of a sudden, he was into postage stamps so light that a breath would blow them away. For a while, he was producing vast, magnificent and ever-changing ink-paintings, and then after that, he was working on strangely disturbing line drawings—where the lines would be sometimes hard, sometimes bold, some-times wild, sometimes flying, deep or cobweb fine. All objects, all styles, all techniques and all materials can be

APPENDIX

used at will... and even squandered. All he wants is to be free.

Spurred on by his imagination, the realm of art is limitless. Just as the globe can support mankind, the minds of each and every one of us can encompass the universe. This is particularly true of the artist's mind. They can use their imagination and creativity because their minds are untrammelled.

The spirit within Meilin's art is absolutely free. This is the reason why his work is so unrestrained and boundless.

Anyone who wants him to be even more eye-catching will help him to become free; anyone who wants to dim his brilliance will bind him and restrain him—but that's impossible—he is like the galloping horses that he paints... He has never had a bridle put on him.

3.

HAN MEILIN CONFOUNDS CRITICS.

This unconventional artist, who leaps from one subject to the next, makes it difficult for critics to take his measure. The composition of his art is too rich and broad. If the connotations of the artwork to be discussed far exceed anything the critic is familiar with, how can he hit this particular nail on the head in his commentary?

In Meilin's artworks of every kind, we can find traces here and there of the aesthetic values of both Chinese and Western art and cultural history. All manner of important achievements in the history of art have served as an inspira-

225

APPENDIX

tion for him—they have not been adopted by him wholesale as a specific aesthetic style, but have instead stolen into the lifeblood of his art. It seems almost like the genes in our bodies.

In my opinion, his art is created from three genetic strands. One is ancient, one is modern and the other comes from Chinese folk-art.

When integrating the aesthetic spirit of Chinese folk-art into modern art, Han Meilin does not consider the style of Chinese folk-art from the perspective of modern Western aesthetics. In their work, Chinese folk have often restricted themselves only to some unique and utterly ossified cultural symbols. In Meilin's paintings, the expressions of these once brilliant folk cultures naturally enter the contemporary era; they are colourful, vulgar, they shout and sing, but like their protagonist, they are alive and kicking in the world of modern art.

At the same time, when we examine the relationship between ancient and modern in Han Meilin's work, we cannot find any trace of influence from the Chinese masters of ink wash painting like Bada Shanren or Shitao, let alone Picasso or Dali. However, the spirit of Chinese freehand brushwork and the sense of modernity are striking. Meilin has turned his back on any aesthetic language that has been elitist and individualised—he is nobody's clone. He has only looked for the origins of art in the sources of both Chinese and Western culture.

I have always thought that ancient art and beautiful folk art can be very naturally integrated with each other, because

APPENDIX

both ancient art and the broad flowering of folk culture draw on the source of all art, the primordial sense of life, and the dawning of civilisation. And isn't this simple and natural cultural life the very thing that our current industrialised civilisation, reliant on machines and computers for communication, yearns for?

Therefore, Han Meilin's art is not only modern and human but also the true soul of the Chinese people.

4.

WHAT CHARACTERS APPEAR IN HAN MEILIN'S WORLD?

As soon as you close your eyes, they appear—the stubborn oxen, crazy horses, elegant deer, crowing roosters, stolid sheep, as well as his delightfully soft baby rabbits and kittens that you just long to touch against your cheek.

In fact, objectively these cannot be considered as Han Meilin's 'subjects' but the temporary focus of his interest. The inherent perseverance, tenacity and frankness in Meilin's nature, and the sudden excitement, delight and tenderness of his heart are all vividly expressed in the creatures that he paints. I have always been able to understand his state of mind from these animals. On the day that we held the ribbon-cutting ceremony for my research institute, Han Meilin gave me an enormous horse, fully two metres tall. That horse was so sturdy and strong, galloping along like a four-legged steam engine. I said to Meilin: "With this kind of vitality, you should live to be over a hundred years old!"

APPENDIX

Everything in Han Meilin's world is an embodiment of his own life. I don't know of anyone else whose art has such a pure sense of liveliness. From time to time, he will pick up a shiny pottery vase or jar with a peculiar shape and say to you: "Look at this globular little thing... isn't it marvellous!" or "See how it has puffed out, isn't it cute?"

This sense of liveliness, moving from representational to abstract, connects every line of drawing in his painting to his strange abstruse symbols.

These are derived from the many unexplained characters found in Han dynasty bamboo slips, ancient pottery, rock paintings, stone carvings, oracle bones and inscriptions on bronze bells, cauldrons and vessels. The reason why they allure him is not only the sense of the historical information lurking mysteriously behind each word, but also the vitality and expressiveness that they have preserved right up to the present day because people in high antiquity used them to convey their thoughts. The reason why Meilin has decided to recreate them is not because of any aesthetic curiosity about these rare ancient characters, nor is he interested in being deliberately mysterious in his visual effects, but because he wants to awaken those remote yet rich symbols of life and symbolic lives.

Every character that appears in Meilin's art is, in fact, none other than himself. Any outstanding artist is highly self-involved. For this reason, everything that appears in this dynamic painter's work is full of vitality—it is rare that anything is static; his excessive emotionalism means that he likes to complete his works in a flash: it is only natural that

228

APPENDIX

he should be so good at spreading ink with a broad brush. An inborn grandeur ensures that each stroke of his calligraphy is as powerful as a leaping tiger. He has no interest in minutiae, he doesn't care about the fuss of interpersonal relationships, and this disinterest in the outside world means that people with their very different characteristics do not impinge upon him. Someone once asked him: "Why don't you paint portraits?"

I was standing right beside him and said: "Portraying people is a writer's job."

5.

WHAT IS THE SOURCE OF HAN MEILIN'S ORIGINALITY?

More than a hundred small porcelain plates hang on a long wall at the Han Meilin Art Museum. There is a small painting at the centre of each of these small plates. Although in each case the picture is different, the birds, rabbits and flowers that he painted there are singing together in various wonderful patterns. When Han Meilin and Zhou Jianping were deeply in love, he got a phone call to say that she was coming to see him: from that moment on, his heart—overflowing with love—began to sing. He was 'singing' all the time that he was painting. All kinds of wonderful images kept flowing from his brush. Love can make people go to the devil or enter a realm of illusion; fantasies are beautiful and the world of fantasy is marvellous indeed. Meilin was completely unable to control himself, and it was not until Jianping pushed open the door and came in that he was finally able to rest his brush. In the space of a single day, he

229

APPENDIX

had painted one hundred and seventy-nine little pictures. These paintings were fired into the hearts of ordinary, thickly glazed porcelain plates, to give concrete and lasting testimony to the artist's love.

Although everybody is willing to enjoy being loved, to love is a happier experience than to be loved. The essence of love is to give it freely. This essence is congruent with the quintessence of art. Because art is not about acquisition; but giving. Love has become the driving force behind Han Meilin's artistic passion. Meilin's love is wide-ranging. He treats friends with love, enthusiasm and generosity, and when it comes to his acquaintances—even complete strangers—he is the same, to the point where he can sometimes seem to be spending money like water. Naturally, this man who loves too much has also often had bitter fruit to eat. More than once I have seen his head bowed in sorrow after falling in love so blindly that he simply danced into a trap. But then afterwards, he forgets all these painful feelings completely and again throws his arms wide to hug those who speak to him in the language of affection. But it is because of this—it is this silliness and self-indulgence in love that keeps new flowers blooming beneath his brush. In fact, no matter how they end up, all that an artist needs are the emotions and inspiration in the moment, even if what that boils down to is mostly his own idealism.

Philosophers seek truth in reality, but artists create magic in illusions.

Is this ultimately down to his nature, or is it because his heart is so full of love that Han Meilin is always doing his

230

best to make his friends happy, to bring happiness to those around him? He is made happy by the happiness of his friends. His art is also happy: you will find no weeping here, no sentimentality and absolutely no obscurity. He has had a number of brushes with the God of Death, but his turbulent life has thrown no shadow on his art—there is only light. He has swallowed the bitterness of life and made honey in his heart: this joy is given to everyone standing before his painting. Meilin is the sunniest painter I have ever met.

The very biggest things do not have shadows. Like the sea and the sky.

However, love will have its own reward. Because of this, he has many friends all over the world and many people who love his art deeply. Today, Han Meilin has already come to epitomise modern Chinese culture and contemporary Chinese art. His symbols have been carried into the clouds on the tail fins of international flights and his Fuwa mascots for the Beijing Olympics have been carried all over the world. Much more to the point, he has created thousands upon thousands of beautiful and wondrous artistic images to spread joy to each and every one of us. So, what exactly does he epitomise? Let me sum it up as follows:

A free spirit, true love, deep foundations, and boundless and magical creativity are all amalgamated into the unique beauty of Han Meilin.

Originally published as the "Introduction" to *The Collected Works of Han Meilin* (2006)

APPENDIX

NONSENSE WRITING

IN THE MOMENT WHEN WE HELD HAN MEILIN's calligraphic masterpiece *Nonsense Writing* in our hands, we witnessed the birth of a work unprecedented in the history of Chinese calligraphy and art history. I was well aware of the exceptional value of this piece in the fields of calligraphy, painting, culture and the history of writing—so during the couple of years when Han Meilin was busy working on it, I kept asking him for updates on his progress. Every time he would cheer me up; sometimes saying: "I'm halfway there... and it's great!" or else: "It's almost finished, and you'll be there for the opening ceremony!"

You might well ask what kind of artwork deserves such avid attention? Open the book that you hold in your hands. Thousands of ancient Chinese characters in every shape and size leap from the page, but when you look more closely, there is not a single one that you recognise. They are odd, mysterious, fantastic and weird... so did Han Meilin just make them up out of nothing? Of course not! They are all characters that were once developed—and indeed used— by our ancestors. They have been preserved to the present day on ancient pottery, on bamboo slips, on wooden plaques, carved onto tortoise shell or bone, inscribed on rocks, chiseled into stone or cast into the surfaces of bronze bells, cauldrons and vessels. Some of them may be variant forms of characters set aside when Li Si organised the standardisation of small seal script at the time of the unification of China under the Qin dynasty, or they may simply be squiggles used by people in antiquity to mark their own property, but their true meaning has long been utterly forgotten.

The history of writing in the early days of mankind is complicated and ever-changing, to the point where it may seem that there simply were no rules. Before a standard orthography was adopted, Chinese characters were highly unstable. There might have been five or six, or even as many as a dozen different ways, to write the name of a single concept or thing, but many of these alternative forms gradually disappeared to the point where modern people simply could not understand them. In much the same way, among the clay tablets covered in cuneiform writing excavated at the Sumerian city of Uruk, or the stone pillars carved with enormous hieroglyphs in Egyptian temples, or the Phaistos Disc discovered on the island of Crete, and Mayan glyphs, you can see many such alien and incomprehensible signs, each one of which is a mystery. However, Meilin could sense a magnificent and magical world full of ancient cultural values in the midst of all this confusion, so he plunged right in, as if bewitched.

The dawn of human civilisation begins with the birth of writing. Since human beings have used writing to record and memorise information, civilisation has become ever deeper and more refined, building on previous achievements. As to how people in antiquity came to think of using written symbols, that is really amazing; and what is even more incredible, the peoples living in various cradles of civilisation around the world came to develop this concept at more or less the same time—writing began some six thou-

APPENDIX

sand years ago. That means that the Yellow Emperor and his official historian Cangjie were not the creators of writing—instead, this was a giant leap for civilisation in the history of mankind!

During the early days of Chinese script, people invented new characters for themselves spontaneously, just as they imagined them, without any restrictions, letting their creativity run free—but this period ended with the unification of China. In the time of the First Emperor, the three important 'grand designs' for unifying the empire were all proposed by Chancellor Li Si. The first of these was encouraging the other kingdoms of the Warring States era to fight against each other; the second was purging dissent through book burning; and the third was the standardisation of the script. The first two of these policies were born of political needs, but the last—creating a standard orthography—represents an enormous contribution to Chinese civilisation.

China occupies a vast area of land with many diverse regions, and differences in dialect pose a real barrier to communication—only the written language has the means to be transmitted unhindered, but that is only because the script has been standardised and formalised. This means that the Qin script reform was of great assistance to the creation of a pan-Chinese culture. But this means that many of the characters and symbols set aside at this time were henceforward no longer used, became forgotten and were lost amidst the sands of time. As a result, they did not reappear in the calligraphic art of later generations.

APPENDIX

These ancient characters may appear obscure, incomprehensible, alien and cold in the eyes of ordinary people, but to Han Meilin, they are emotional, expressive, living symbols. As a result, caring for, studying, experiencing these lost ancient characters and bringing them back to life has become an important part of Meilin's artistic career. It has taken thirty years for him to assemble the ancient script forms seen in this book, *Nonsense Writing*. He has collected as many as thirty thousand individual words from ancient pottery, bronze vessel inscriptions, stone carvings, and archeological reports. And today, these ancient characters appear alive and well in his *Nonsense Writing*, in their multifarious forms.

It is a truism in the history of art to say that "calligraphy and painting are of the same origin" but has anyone ever suggested that writing and painting are of the same origin?

Painters like to think that painting and calligraphy are linked, but it is a historical fact that writing and painting are also fundamentally connected at source.

When people in antiquity recorded something, they began by drawing its shape. The earliest words are pictorial and the earliest paintings convey the meaning of words. Aren't pictographs the most ancient of all human writing systems? Chinese characters have a pictographic base too. Although they have undergone continuous evolution, right up to the present day the painting gene is visible in ever-changing characters in their writing grid, and this is also the fundamental reason why they can be transformed into the unique art form of Chinese calligraphy. Therefore, the

APPENDIX

understanding that writing and painting share the same origin has become the historical justification and cultural basis for Han Meilin's book, *Nonsense Writing*.

However, instead of simply reproducing these forgotten ancient characters, Meilin has imbued them with his own individual spirit; across great distances of space and time, he has listened to and questioned the basic thinking and imaginings of those peoples from long-ago, as well as allowing them their own originality and creative freedom. This is in spite of not being able to decipher the original meaning of every ancient character—and he certainly does not want to become caught up in the painstaking work of etymologists. With the unique sensitivity of an artist, he understands the fundamental spirit and beauty of humankind.

Of course, you can also find Han Meilin's distinctive sense of aesthetics here.

This beauty comes from his personality: dignified, vigorous, frank, free and inexhaustibly passionate. Is his natural personality somehow similar to the original temperament of these archaic Chinese characters? Anyway, I can no longer distinguish whether it is the ancient characters that have had a significant influence on him, or whether his artistic temperament has been more important.

As a painter, Han Meilin's calligraphy is highly painterly. When he transformed these etymologically rich ancient characters into calligraphic art in his *Nonsense Writing*, his aesthetic sense, sensitivity to imagery and infinite creativity in visual forms were naturally integrated into it.

236

He has taken a clear decision to integrate painting with calligraphy, so as to make calligraphy more visually attractive, formal and painterly. If we did not have such a magical artist as Han Meilin, how could we have such a marvellous work of art as *Nonsense Writing*?

Nonsense Writing is a great work of philology. For the first time, Han Meilin has collected together these individual words, scattered to the four winds since antiquity, and restored them to calligraphy. This means that *Nonsense Writing* is first and foremost a thesaurus of ancient writing, documenting more than ten thousand archaic characters. Its sheer size demonstrates the infinite cultural creativity of our ancestors. Han Meilin seems to have brought us to the very source of five thousand years of Chinese civilisation. Stand here and look out into the distance, and you will see tens of thousands of ancient characters glittering all the way to the horizon, like the waves of the sea.

Nonsense Writing is a unique and wonderful masterpiece of calligraphy. An artist's love has served to revive one by one these archaic Chinese characters that almost passed from our history; they are strange and yet familiar, mysterious and intimate, profound and close, alien and beautiful. After all his hard work, he has seen the rebirth of beauty.

I am sure that *Nonsense Writing* will be recognised as one of Han Meilin's masterpieces. This is not just because of its importance in textual history, calligraphy and cultural history, but because this is the ultimate expression of Han Meilin's life's work.

What is its significance?

APPENDIX

God created Han Meilin, and Han Meilin created *Nonsense Writing*.

Originally published as the "Introduction" to Han Meilin's calligraphic collection *Nonsense Writing* (2006)

IMAGIST LANDSCAPES

HAN MEILIN ALWAYS LIKES TO GIVE YOU A TURN.

When I say he "likes to give you a turn" I am not talking about trying to be outrageous, taking risks or seeking to appall people deliberately. This is in reference to his originality and creativity, his unusual imagination, the manifestations of which so far exceed anything that you thought he could possibly do—a natural born genius.

Can Han Meilin paint landscape paintings? If you ask people, they will just ask you back: "Has Han Meilin painted any landscapes?" No, but just now he has placed a book of his landscape paintings in my hands that weighs as much as a stone slab.

To be honest, I have never seen this kind of landscape painting before. There is no focal point, no realistic or exact representation, none of the rich strokes or sweeps of dry ink, pointillism or washes that we associate with traditional Chinese landscape painting techniques, none of the scenes familiar to people in antiquity or people today. Nevertheless, these pictures allow me to feel the dazzle of mountains in the sunshine, and their majestic, cold peaks in the shade; there are also hazy clouds, silent, empty valleys, little

238

saplings growing quietly on steep cliffs, and birds chirruping away for some unknown reason... However, none of these things are actually depicted, set down, represented, or in any way clearly shown. Look! Here you have great blobs of colour, there you have broad strokes of ink—put together you have a textured surface that seems rubbed and splashed at will, with wet paint and ink allowed to pool on the rice paper essentially at random. And yet, all kinds of wonderful vistas seem to emerge in this way.

At the moment, critics seem to be fixated upon the question of rigid genre categorisations...

What kind of landscape painting is this? Is it in the Song or Yuan dynasty style? Is this literati painting? Freehand brushwork? Or is it a Western-style abstract piece? Sorry, it is none of them.

Traditional Chinese art is representational, while modern Western painting is abstract. Han Meilin's landscapes are neither representational nor abstract. So, what is it? Don't forget that the Chinese people also have the concept of 'imagism'.

'Vision' or *yi* is an important feature of Chinese culture.

For example, we have the concept of the 'visionary realm'. There is only realm in Western painting, that is, spatial imagery. However, Chinese painting, especially landscape painting, pays great attention to the visionary realm, and even makes this the standard by which we judge the quality of a painting. The so-called 'visionary realm' that is so important to Chinese people means that artists attempt to

APPENDIX

integrate meaning (that is, ideas, connotations, poetics, feelings, taste) into their spatial imagery, so that it is no longer just a matter of visual aesthetics but an intense emotional experience. In a similar vein, images in Chinese art have a deeper layer of meaning, in their 'imagist' painting. However, imagist art is not abstract, nor is it entirely representational—it sits somewhere between the two. In order to express their vision even more freely and fully, this artistic movement eschews portrayal and descriptiveness, and refuses to be limited by the conventions of representational art, nor does it allow visual perception to confine the imagination. In this sense, can we not say that Han Meilin's landscape paintings are imagist landscapes?

We can see just this kind of imagist landscape painting in the works of the four monastic painters of the early Qing dynasty—Shitao, Bada Shanren, Kun Can and Hong Ren; in Zen painting and freehand brushwork; from the 'raindrop' texture strokes found in the paintings of Mi Fu and his son, Mi Youren, to the dripped ink of Huang Binhong, but most of these are partial utilisations of this style, while Han Meilin's landscapes are imagist in their entirety.

This is precisely because Han Meilin's perspective has been formed by the imagist tradition so significant in the history of Chinese culture, and not Western abstraction. His landscape paintings are imbued with Chinese qualities, while at the same time rich in their modernist spirit.

Creativity often comes upon Han Meilin in a frenzy, and thus he hurled himself into landscape painting like a bison charging. Entirely inadvertently, he has put forward a new research topic for those studying the development of landscape painting. Yet again, he has given all of us a turn, and suddenly I began to wonder: "Is there anything he cannot paint?"

Let this be an introduction.

Originally published as the "Introduction" to Han Meilin's painting collection *Chewing Mountains and Swallowing Rivers* (2011).

TRIBUTE TO A GREAT ARTIST

FIRST OF ALL, I would like to say a few words on behalf of Han Meilin's closest friends. We would like to explain that every time he holds an exhibition, we don't all come at once. Instead, we arrive as soon as we hear the news and then race away to discuss our thoughts—we turn up uninvited, having arranged to meet at the exhibition, prepared to receive yet another shock from this artist. But no matter how ready you may think you are, Han Meilin will give you a surprise greater than you could possibly have imagined. What is stronger than the surprise is the shock.

I remember that ten years ago, Han Meilin held an exhibition in the National Art Museum of China, with almost three thousand works filling eleven halls. This time, the National Museum of China has provided him with 6,000 square metres, and yet again they have been filled, but of course, this is far from being the totality of his creative achievements during this last decade. Who else could fill such a huge exhibition space with his work? Probably only Tan

APPENDIX

Lihua and his Beijing Symphony Orchestra could fill this space with sound.

Han Meilin's art has always been filled with great individuality and creative tension, and it allows us to read the great depth of history and the seeds of traditional culture sown in ancient rock art and pottery, Western Zhou bronzes, Han lacquerware and pictorial carvings, the statuary of the Northern and Southern dynasties, the murals of the High Tang, and the ceramics of the Song.

In the past hundred years, due to the collision between China and the West, artists have painfully explored how Eastern and Western cultures define themselves through conflict, and in the last thirty years or so since the opening up of China, modernism has introduced new topics and challenges to Chinese artists. In this regard, Han Meilin's bold and creative efforts must be faced up to and dealt with by critics.

We should agree that Han Meilin is a contemporary artist of rare talent.

The essence of art is expressed through life force and vital creativity. Creativity comes from the imagination. On one occasion, Han Meilin and I attended a boring meeting. Once the meeting began, Han Meilin opened his sketch pad and leaned over to tell me: "I'm going to draw oxen!" Straight away he began to draw all kinds of cattle—docile, stubborn, proud, sleepy, and so on. Some looked as if they came off a Han dynasty pictorial brick, while others were in the style of ancient bronzes, rock art or a folk art paper-cut... The meeting lasted more than an hour, and in that time he had drawn more than three hundred different oxen, and if the meeting hadn't finished when it did, he'd still be drawing. What kind of creativity is this, and where does it come from? I looked at him, and suddenly a line from *Hamlet* came to mind: "I could be bounded in a nut shell and count myself a king of infinite space."

What is genius? What is the secret of genius? I've always wanted to find an answer, and now I have—the secret of genius is genius; it is innate, independent and unrepeatable; genius is such that the world gains from its presence and loses from its absence. That is why I have said to Han Meilin: "You are a natural born genius."

Let us now talk about Han Meilin the man.

He is someone who lives for truth and sincerity, and lives to love—of course, this is a very happy *modus vivendi*. The thing I have always most admired about him is his ignorance of the ways of the world.

He is terrible at mathematics, so he cannot do business. Since he has no interest whatsoever in material success, and is always driven by his feelings, he has ended up giving most of his paintings away. He hates any kind of cruelty or nastiness, and is neither restrained by the occasion nor turned from his path by any considerations of status, so he often ends up in quarrels in which he offends people. But what else do we expect from such a great artist? I think of Goethe's famous saying: "Only the sun has a right to its spots."

APPENDIX

Those of us who are Han Meilin's friends have one thing in common with each other. We all regard admiring other people's good qualities as a kind of happiness. There is a huge difference in height between myself and Han Meilin, since I am thirty-five centimetres taller than him, so when we are standing next to each other, I am forced to look down on him. However, in my heart, I have always looked up to him.

At this moment, he demands—yet again—that I look up to him.

Today, all the friends attending this exhibition of Han Meilin's paintings have asked me to tell him: you are free, you can do whatever you want, but please look after yourself and don't work too hard. Make sure you take time to relax, don't bother with these endless meetings, make sure you eat properly and don't forget your medications, so that when you are fully rested and filled with energy, you can create even more wonderful paintings and even greater beauty for us all to enjoy.

An impromptu speech given at the opening ceremony of the exhibition: *The Art of Han Meilin* (2011).

REMARKS AT THE OPENING CEREMONY OF THE HAN MEILIN ART MUSEUM IN BEIJING

GOOD EVENING, LADIES AND GENTLEMEN! Today, many of the artists present, not just myself, are counted among the good friends and indeed confidantes of Han Meilin.

APPENDIX

Everyone regards Meilin as a child—a grown-up child. This is because he has preserved his childlike frankness and wilfulness, as well as his childlike sincerity, in spite of the many vicissitudes of fate. He is not on his guard against anyone, and all day, every day his mind is filled with illusions.

A man like Han Meilin, such a great artist... how can he possibly be a child?

Can a child take over such a huge building—the Han Meilin Art Museum of Beijing? Can a child fill it with thousands of astonishing, even shocking works of art? Can a child paint the vermillion phoenix that Han Meilin designed for the tails of the Air China planes flying around in the sky? Can a child make the Fuwa mascots that you can see everywhere in China nowadays? Or how about those gigantic sculptures that Han Meilin designed, tens or even hundreds of metres high, which we can see every time we travel up and down the Yangtze River?

Where does Han Meilin derive such towering creativity from?

Is it love for the Earth? Is it his passion for art? Or a demand for beauty?

At the press conference at the Great Hall of the People for the publication of Han Meilin's book, *Nonsense Writing*, I said: "I can spend all day with Han Meilin but he still remains a mystery to me." I have always wondered whether Han Meilin has some kind of artistic nuclear energy: he uses his explosive energy to complete at least one thousand

APPENDIX

outstanding works of art a year. Han Meilin's artistic realm can sometimes seem limitless—at one and the same time highly modern, and yet still informed by the aesthetic spirit and cultural energies of ancient and folk art. Few artists can claim to have worked in so many genres—ceramics, sculpture, calligraphy, painting and design. Yet Han Meilin has plunged into all these fields to achieve extraordinary success.

When I speak of these things, I feel that we can no longer consider Han Meilin as a child. He is an artistic giant of our time—a giant at one metre seventy. When standing with Han Meilin, because I am too tall, I have to look down at him but in my heart, I have always looked up to my wonderful friend. Enjoying and appreciating your friends is also a kind of happiness. I am sure that many of the artists here today will look at Han Meilin with appreciative eyes, and love him as much as I do.

However, I would like to take this opportunity to remind him that he is now seventy-two years old. In terms of life-span, seventy-two is nothing to sneeze at; but when it comes to his spirit and art, it does not matter whether he lives to be seventy, eighty or ninety, Han Meilin will always be forty, thirty, twenty... or maybe even younger—a loveable, extraordinary child.

That is all I have to say. Thank you!

(June 25, 2008)

APPENDIX

REMARKS AT THE OPENING CEREMONY OF THE HAN MEILIN ART MUSEUM IN HANGZHOU

As a friend of Han Meilin, and on behalf of those who have travelled here from Beijing today, I am very proud to stand here. So many people have come to join us, the flights must have been packed, and among contemporary artists at work in China today, I imagine that only Han Meilin could have packed out every flight. What is it about Meilin that makes him such a draw? I guess that it is partly the interest we feel in his art, and partly the personal charm that all of us have experienced. Each one of us is numbered among his satellites. We go wherever Han Meilin holds an exhibition. Why? It is because every work of art that he produces is fresh. He never repeats himself. These pieces come bursting out of his own existence. He is like an atomic reaction in constant fission, ceaselessly regenerating himself, overflowing with inspiration. Han Meilin's imagination is incredible, and his creativity is astounding. It is for this reason that he often says that he hasn't even really begun yet.

Every artist is a mystery. The only part of the mystery that is Han Meilin that we can explain is his passion for life, nature, people, friends and beauty. Passion is the driving force for all art, and love is another... but this is something that only Zhou Jianping knows. We can envy the people of Hangzhou: they are blessed in this way because Han Meilin's wife comes from this city. But I don't understand quite how Hangzhou people have managed to turn this human marriage into a marvellous conjunction; how, in constructing this museum, they have integrated a kind of

247

APPENDIX

artistic beauty with these surroundings of outstanding natural beauty, as well as historical and cultural significance. Walking in, I was surprised and amazed by its scale and artistic brilliance. It is like the Mogao caves of Dunhuang, but created by a single individual. His art has brought greater glory to the cultural life of Hangzhou and has given a new gloss to the civilisation of this region. Therefore, we are happy that Han Meilin's art can blossom and bear fruit here. I hope that Meilin will cherish his health as his friends do, for if he can stay well and keep his spirits intact, his art will only become more beautiful, and this golden age can endure for even longer.

(October 19, 2005)

REMARKS AT THE OPENING CEREMONY OF THE HAN MEILIN ART MUSEUM IN YINCHUAN

TODAY, MANY GOOD FRIENDS, and many friends from the art world, and indeed a great number of our finest contemporary writers, artists, scholars and experts from all over the country have come to join us here. At a time when the winter solstice is approaching and the coldest time of the year draws close, we have come here to find a kind of warmth. This feeling of warmth, sincerity and wonder is derived from the sense of fellowship that we share with our host today: Han Meilin.

Another element that has brought us here is our shared love of culture. As we all know, the great Helan mountain rock paintings have inspired Han Meilin's art and given rise

APPENDIX

to much of his work. Today, the Han Meilin Art Museum stands right at this source of inspiration. Who else would have dared to put a museum down in this great wilderness? Here we have an artist who has travelled all over the world, who has nevertheless returned to embrace his origins. This has moved us all deeply—this is indeed a warm feeling.

This touches upon what we might call 'gratitude'—gratitude for art and gratitude for culture. Who has such a great sense of thankfulness? Who is capable of such generosity of gesture? Just moments ago, we were admiring the more than a thousand works of art housed in this museum, and each painting, each sculpture is the result of painstaking effort, an expression of a lifetime of hard-won skill. Thers pieces have been brought here, sent back to the source of his inspiration... this shows his true love for the culture of his motherland and is a manifestation of the deep feelings and love that all artists and writers have for the culture in which they were raised. If all of our people and those in charge of all aspects of society had such a sincere love of culture, we would not have to worry about the future, for our country's future prosperity would be assured.

For more than a hundred years in China, our cultural and artistic circles—particularly the world of the fine arts—has been looking for a language: the artistic language of modern China. Now Han Meilin has given us a revelation—a wonderful moment of enlightenment. From this museum, we can see that here, history is not dead, it has been brought back to life by Han Meilin's personality and artistic talent. Han Meilin is a small man but an artist of towering abilities. His art is produced at such a high rate, so quickly, he is too

249

APPENDIX

wild, too reckless—sometimes we just want him to take a break, leave himself a little more space; but then at other times, we want him to paint more, bring more beauty to this world. Therefore, we all hope that Han Meilin will look after himself, eat better food, sleep more deeply, waste less time in pointless bureaucracy and spend more time painting, for if you give full play to your talents, you will surely be rewarded with health and longevity.

Bless you, Han Meilin! Let us all congratulate Han Meilin!

(December 21, 2015)

THE HAN MEILIN ART MUSEUM AT YINCHUAN

FOR A TREE TO GROW HUNDREDS OF FEET TALL it must be deeply rooted in the earth; for a river to flow a thousand miles it must be connected to its source. Han Meilin has long been profoundly influenced by the ancient rock art here, and now the Helan mountains will be rewarded by this great artist. A thousand masterpieces inspired by these rock paintings are hereby gratefully presented to you—when has there ever been such a munificent benefaction? This is an important cultural legacy, as well as a magnificent artistic achievement. Accordingly, the Yinchuan Municipal People's Government has decided to build this Han Meilin Art Museum within the confines of the Helan Mountain Rock Art Heritage Park, so that these treasures can be preserved and displayed in perpetuity, to be seen by the public and studied by academics.

250

APPENDIX

The Yinchuan branch of the Han Meilin Art Museum was opened to the public on 21 December 2015. This museum is the third in China to be dedicated solely to displaying Han Meilin's paintings, after those in Hangzhou and Beijing, with an area of 15,868 square metres, of which 6,694 square metres is occupied by the museum itself: this contains five large halls, two smaller rooms, one corridor exhibition area and one open space, which serve to display the full range of Han Meilin's works inspired by rock art, including paintings, calligraphy, sculpture, ceramics and textile art. These pieces will not only enable people in the northwest to enjoy original works by Han Meilin and to admire his abundant creativity and multifarious achievements, but also to reflect on the Helan mountain rock art close at hand. Here we can see a living connection between an ancient civilisation and contemporary art, and feel the long history and constant development of Chinese culture.

This is a wonderful gift and deeply meaningful—it deserves to be remembered.

August 20, 2015

ENDNOTES

FOREWORD

1. Zhang Xianliang (1936-2014) was a Chinese novelist, essayist, poet and former president of the Chinese Writers Association of Ningxia autonomous region of China. During the Anti-Rightist Movement (1957-1959), he was branded as a counter-revolutionary and sent to a labour camp at the age of 21 in 1957.'
2. Feng Mu (1919-1995), also known as Feng Xianzhi, was a Chinese writer born in Beijing and served as the Vice President of the Chinese Writers Association (CWA).
3. David Dubal is an American pianist, author, broadcaster, painter and lecturer who authored dozens of essays and articles.

1. OVERTURE OF SUFFERING

1. Mao Zedong started 'The Great Leap Forward (1958-1962)' in China and asked everybody to collect iron ore from anywhere including old bicycles etc. His aim was to overtake Britain in steel production which was super ambitious at that time.
2. The Socialist Education Movement which is also known as the 'Four Clean-Ups' (to cleanse politics, economics, organisation and ideology), was a movement launched by Mao Zedong in 1963 and it continued until 1966. "
3. 'Three Red Banners' or the 'Three Red Flags' was a slogan started in the late 1950s which called for a 'General Line for Socialist Construction', 'The Great Leap Forward' and 'The People's Communes'.
4. Hefei is the capital city of Anhui province.
5. Struggle sessions were held during the Cultural Revolution where the so-called 'accused' were put on a stage and everybody denounced or criticised their acts with them having almost no chance to defend themselves. They used to be held in a prominent place and people in the area were notified in advance so that the maximum number of people could attend. These sessions were so humiliating that many intellectuals and artists in China committed suicide after this.

ENDNOTES

6. After the grain rationing system was introduced in China from the 1950s to 1985, people were given grain coupons to buy a certain amount of food at lower, state-imposed and controlled prices to control food production and boost industrialisation.

7. *'Comprehensive Mirror in Aid of Governance'* which is famously known as *Zizhi Tongjian* in Chinese (資治通鑑) was published in 1084 and is a pioneering reference book in Chinese historiography. The book records Chinese history from 403 BC to 959 AD in three million Chinese characters and 249 volumes.

8. 'Reform through labour', is a slogan of the Chinese criminal justice system and has been used to refer to the use of penal labour and prison farms in the People's Republic of China.

9. Bengbu is a city in Anhui which is also nicknamed Pearl City.

10. Among Han Meilin's famous paintings, is a portrait of a cute dog entitled *Friend in Adversity*. His paintings of animals are quite loveable, and they attract huge attention.

11. Zhou Keqin (1937-1990) was a writer and considered as a leading figure of scar literature in China.

12. Big-character posters are handwritten large wall-mounted posters, used as a means of communication for protest, propaganda and popular communications.

13. 'Rehabilitation' was a process in which those who had fallen into disgrace would get restored to normal life during the Cultural Revolution period.

14. Gai Jiaotian (1888-1971) was a Beijing Opera artist and was most famous for his role as Wu Song, a fictional hero in one of the four most famous classics of China, *The Water Margin*.

15. KMT (Kuomintang), a political party now based in Taiwan, and the CPC (the Communist Party of China - now the ruling party of China) were engaged in a fierce power struggle before 1949.

16. *Sketches of a Three-Family Village* was the name of an essay column published in a Beijing newspaper from 1961 to 1966 by three authors, namely Deng Tuo (1911-1966) who committed suicide due to persecution during the Cultural Revolution, Wu Han (1909-1969) who may also have committed suicide during the Cultural Revolution, and Liao Mosha. All three writers were accused of being anti-CPC and persecuted cruelly. Only Liao Mosha survived the trauma of the Cultural Revolution and died in 1990.

17. The Four Reactionary Writers were Yang Hansheng (1902-1993), Tian Han (1898-1968) who died due to persecution during the Cultural Revolution, Xia Yan (1900-1995) and Zhou Yang (1908-1989). The four were also founders of the League of Left-Wing Writers in 1930.

ENDNOTES

18. 'Shame parading' on the streets was a mode of public humiliation during the Cultural Revolution.

19. The Three Green Group was formed on 9 July 1938 under the leadership of KMT party leader Chiang Kai-shek in Wuchang. The 'Three Green Group' was the youth organ of the KMT.

20. Ba Jin (1904-2005) was a famous Chinese author and political activist, best known for his work *Family*.

21. Ms Zhang Zhixin was a dissident during the Cultural Revolution who was incarcerated and finally executed for opposing the party despite being a member of the party.

22. Professor Feng Jicai published this book in 2003 which depicted the arduous journey of a hundred common Chinese people during the Cultural Revolution period.

23. A "supreme instruction" was any instruction or order issued by Mao (or by senior party organs in his name), regarded as "supreme" because they could not be questioned. Whatever Mao said at the height of the Cultural Revolution was regarded as "unquestionable".

2. HISTORY OF PURGATORY

1. *Taijiquan* or *Tai Ji* is an internal Chinese martial art practiced for both its defence training and health benefits.

2. Cong Weixi (1933-) is a contemporary Chinese author and was branded as a 'Rightist' during the Cultural Revolution period.

3. May Seventh Cadre School was where leftists politically persecuted intellectuals during the Cultural Revolution.

4. 'Offence by Pen and Defence by Sword' was a call given by Jiang Qing (Wife of Mao Zedong and a prominent member of the Gang of Four) on 22 July 1967 to not only attack the counter-revolutionaries through writing but in the act of defence they could also use weapons and even kill people. Front page editorial articles in support of this were published in several newspapers.

5. A book comprising famous speeches and writing of Chairman Mao, also known in the West as the '*Little Red Book*'. The book contains almost 427 quotations, organised thematically into 33 chapters.

6. Mo Yan, a novelist who won the Nobel Prize for Literature in 2012.

7. The Criticise Lin (Biao), Criticise Confucius campaign (批林批孔 *pilin pikong*) was a political propaganda campaign started by Mao Zedong and his wife, Jiang Qing, the leader of the Gang of Four. It lasted from 1973 until the end of the Cultural Revolution in 1976.

8. 1600-1100 BC.

ENDNOTES

3. RETURNING TO THE HUMAN WORLD AGAIN

1. Huangmei opera is one of the most famous and mainstream operas in China.
2. *The Legend of Tianyun Mountain* is a novel which was the basis for a film made in 1980 about Chinese people's sufferings from the long-term political campaigns from '"Anti-Rightists'" in the 1950s until the fall of the Gang of Four.
3. Chang Shuhong (1904-1994) was a famous Chinese painter, known as the 'Guardian of Dunhuang' and publicised the ancient art works at the Mogao caves of Dunhuang.
4. Chang Shana is the daughter of Chang Shuhong, and like her father is famous for dedicating her life to preserving and promoting the art of Dunhuang.
5. Confucius was also born in Shandong province.
6. Aleksey Nikolayevich Tolstoy; 10 January 1883 – 23 February 1945), was a Russian writer who wrote in many genres but specialised in science fiction and historical novels.

CONVERSATIONS IN THE KINGDOM OF ART

1. Gao Minglu (1940-) is an art critic who researched at Harvard and currently teaches at an American University.

1. AN INQUEST INTO THE KINGDOM OF ART

1. '"九朽一罳'" or '"Nine Immortals'", refers to a technique of drawing characters, and later to a serious attitude in literary and artistic creation.
2. *The Six Fundamental Principles of Chinese Paintings* were established by Xie He in *Six Points to Consider when Judging a Painting* from the preface to his book *The Record of the Classification of Old Painters* (古畫品錄) written circa 550 and refers to 'old' and 'ancient' practices.
3. Qi Baishi (1864-1957), born in Hunan province, was a famous Chinese painter, noted for the whimsical, often playful style of his watercolour

256

ENDNOTES

works.

4. *Qinqiang* or *Luantan* is the representative folk Chinese opera of the northwest province of Shaanxi, known as the State of Qin thousands of years ago.
5. Jean-Baptiste Poquelin (1622-1673), known by his stage name Molière, died after performing on stage. His influence is such that the French language itself is often referred to as the "Language of Molière".
6. Daoxuan (Wu Daozi; 680 – 760) was a famous Chinese artist of the Tang dynasty.
7. Wu Guanzhong (29 August 1919 – 25 June 2010) was a contemporary Chinese painter widely recognised as a founder of modern Chinese painting.
8. (221-206 BC).
9. Yan Zhenqing (709-785) was the leading calligrapher of the Tang dynasty.
10. In Buddhism, the term anattā or anātman refers to the doctrine of 'non-self', that there is no unchanging, permanent self, soul or essence in phenomena.

2. TRICOLOUR

1. (960-1279).
2. Wang Xizhi (303-361) is considered as one of the greatest Chinese calligraphers.
3. Huaisu (737-799) was a famous Buddhist cursive calligrapher and was admired by many including the famous Tang poet Li Bai .
4. Chinese bronze inscriptions comprise writing on bronze bells and other such artefacts from the second millennium BC to the fourth century BC.
5. Mao Gong Ding is a bronze vessel of Western Zhou (around 700 BC) period and is currently kept in Taipei.
6. The Daoguang Emperor (16 September 1782 – 26 February 1850) was the eighth Emperor of the Qing dynasty, and the sixth Qing emperor to rule over China properly, reigning from 1820 to 1850.
7. (618-907).
8. (960-1279).
9. The Ming dynasty ruled China from 1368 to 1644 while the Qing ruled from 1644 to 1911.
10. The May Fourth Movement was an anti-imperialist, cultural and political movement which grew out of student protests in Beijing on 4 May 1919.

ENDNOTES

11. Pavel Petrovich Chistyakov (1832-1919), a Russian painter and art teacher known for historical and genre scenes as well as portraits.

3. FOUR BROTHERS

1. Li Keran (1907-1989), a famous Chinese painter and one of the most valued painters in the Chinese art market. Some of his paintings have been sold for millions of dollars. He also propounded that all paintings should have a 'soul'. A book was also published in 2012 in his name with the same motto of *Paintings Having a Soul* (in Chinese only)'.
2. Yan Zhenqing (709-785) was a Chinese calligrapher of the Tang dynasty whose works are often imitated.
3. Liu Gongquan (778-865) was a brilliant Chinese calligrapher, famous for regular scripts in Chinese. He was also a follower of Yan Zhenqing's script.
4. Zhao Mengfu (1254-1322) was a Chinese scholar and famous painter of the Yuan dynasty.
5. Qi Gong (1912-2005) was a renowned Chinese calligrapher and artist.
6. Seal script (Chinese: 篆 書 *zhuanshu*) is an ancient style of writing Chinese characters that was common throughout the latter half of the first millennium BC.
7. The *Prajñāpāramitā Sutras* are "a collection of about forty texts", composed somewhere on the Indian subcontinent between approximately 100 BC and 600 AD
8. Guan Gong (who died in 220 AD) was a military general who served under warlord Liu Bei and is worshipped as a divine figure in Chinese folklore.
9. (550-577 AD)
10. Qian Shaowu (1928-) is a famous Chinese artist, who was born in Wuxi, Jiangxi province.
11. The Northern Zhou dynasty (北周 *Bei Zhou*) followed the Western Wei and ruled northern China from 557 to 581 AD
12. 'Three-Star Mound' is the name of an archaeological site and a major Bronze Age culture in modern Guanghan, Sichuan, China.
13. With a length of 78 metres and a height of 15.8 metres, it is the longest bronze sculpture in the world. It used 140 tons of bronze and was officially completed in July 2004.
14. In the Warring States period (475-222 BC), workers made a lot of armour and weapons made of bronze.
15. Yixing clay teapots, also called purple sand teapots, are made from clay produced near Yixing in the eastern Chinese province of Jiangsu.

258

ENDNOTES

4. ONE MAN'S MOGAO CAVES

1. The Two Sessions refers to the annual plenary sessions of the National People's Congress (NPC) and the National Committee of the Chinese People's Political Consultative Conference (CPPCC).
2. Liu Shikun (Born on 8 March 1939) is a famous Chinese composer and pianist.
3. In the original Chinese book, it was mistakenly written as a film from Pakistan, but the translator contacted artist Han Meilin and he clarified that the film was indeed Indian and not from Pakistan. The film 'Caravan' was a blockbuster Bollywood film made in 1971 and was the highest grossing foreign film in China when it was released there in 1979.

ABOUT THE AUTHOR

Feng Jicai is a contemporary author, artist and cultural scholar who rose to prominence as a pioneer of China's Scar Literature movement that emerged after the Cultural Revolution. He has published almost a hundred literary works in China and more than forty internationally. He is proficient in both Chinese and Western artistic techniques and his artwork has been exhibited in China, Japan, the US, Singapore and Austria. He has had a major influence on contemporary Chinese society with his work on the Project to Save Chinese Folk Cultural Heritages and his roles as honorary member of the Literature and Arts Association, honorary president of the China Folk Literature and Art Association and adviser to the State Council, among others. He is also dean, professor and PhD supervisor at the Feng Jicai Institute of Literature and Art, Tianjin University.

ABOUT THE TRANSLATOR
YUKTESHWAR KUMAR

Dr Yukteshwar Kumar is a well-known sinologist and the first-ever South Asian Deputy Mayor of the UNESCO heritage city of Bath, UK of Asian and non-white descent. He is a senior academic at the University of Bath and researched at Peking University as a Nehru Fellow. While researching in China, he received guidance from the well-known professor and former vice-chancellor of the university, Professor Ji Xianlin. He has taught at several Indian and Chinese universities.

Dr Kumar is also a prolific writer and has written dozens of articles in Bengali, Chinese, English and Hindi, and published his opinion pieces in global media outlets such as *BBC* online, *People's Daily*, *China Daily* and *The Hindustan Times*. He has also translated this book into Hindi and Bengali.

ABOUT THE TRANSLATOR
OLIVIA MILBURN

Olivia Milburn is a professor of Chinese language and literature at Seoul National University. She was first drawn to Chinese literature after reading an English translation of the classic novel, *The Dream of the Red Chamber* by Cao Xueqin. She has authored several books including *Cherishing Antiquity: The Cultural Construction of an Ancient Chinese Kingdom*, *The Spring and Autumn Annals of Master Yan* and *Urbanization in Early and Medieval China: Gazetteers for the City of Suzhou*. In collaboration with Christopher Payne, she has translated two spy novels by Mai Jia, including the bestselling *Decoded*, from Chinese to English.

About Sinoist Books

We hope you enjoyed these insights into Han Meilin's life, from the Cultural Revolution to his rise to artistic eminence.

SINOIST BOOKS brings the best of Chinese fiction to English-speaking readers. We aim to create a greater understanding of Chinese culture and society, and to provide an outlet for the ideas and creativity of the country's most talented authors.

To let us know what you thought of this book, or to learn more about the diverse range of exciting Chinese fiction in translation we publish, find us online. If you're as passionate about Chinese literature as we are, then we'd love to hear your thoughts!

www.sinoistbooks.com / *@sinoistbooks*